Cambridge Elements

Elements in the Problems of God
edited by
Michael L. Peterson
Asbury Theological Seminary

THE PROBLEM OF GOD IN BUDDHISM

Signe Cohen
University of Missouri

CAMBRIDGE
UNIVERSITY PRESS

CAMBRIDGE
UNIVERSITY PRESS

Shaftesbury Road, Cambridge CB2 8EA, United Kingdom

One Liberty Plaza, 20th Floor, New York, NY 10006, USA

477 Williamstown Road, Port Melbourne, VIC 3207, Australia

314–321, 3rd Floor, Plot 3, Splendor Forum, Jasola District Centre, New Delhi – 110025, India

103 Penang Road, #05–06/07, Visioncrest Commercial, Singapore 238467

Cambridge University Press is part of Cambridge University Press & Assessment, a department of the University of Cambridge.

We share the University's mission to contribute to society through the pursuit of education, learning and research at the highest international levels of excellence.

www.cambridge.org
Information on this title: www.cambridge.org/9781009578707

DOI: 10.1017/9781009269223

When citing this work, please include a reference to the DOI 10.1017/9781009269223

First published 2025

A catalogue record for this publication is available from the British Library

ISBN 978-1-009-57870-7 Hardback
ISBN 978-1-009-26918-6 Paperback
ISSN 2754-8724 (online)
ISSN 2754-8716 (print)

The Problem of God in Buddhism

Elements in the Problems of God

DOI: 10.1017/9781009269223
First published online: March 2025

Signe Cohen
University of Missouri

Author for correspondence: Signe Cohen, cohens@missouri.edu

Abstract: Since Buddhism does not include a belief in a personal god instrumental to the creation of the world or to human salvation, it is often assumed that gods play no part in Buddhism at all. This Element complicates the simplistic assessment of Buddhism as an "atheistic religion" and discusses the various roles deities play in Buddhist texts and practice. *The Problem of God in Buddhism* includes a comprehensive analysis of the Buddhist refutations of a creator God, the idea of salvation without divine intervention, the role of minor deities in Buddhism, the question of whether Buddhas and Bodhisattvas can function as gods in certain forms of Buddhism, and the notion of the sacred as apart from the divine in Buddhist traditions.

Keywords: Buddhism, gods, atheism, atheistic religion, salvation

ISBNs: 9781009578707 (HB), 9781009269186 (PB), 9781009269223 (OC)
ISSNs: 2754-8724 (online), 2754-8716 (print)

Contents

1 Buddhism as "Atheism"? 1

2 Buddhism and the Idea of a Divine Creator 13

3 Salvation without Gods 23

4 The Roles of Gods, Buddhas, and Bodhisattvas 34

5 Gods and Goddesses in Buddhism 40

6 The Sacred in Buddhism 53

References 63

1 Buddhism as "Atheism"?

What Is Buddhism?

The Buddhist tradition originated in northern India around the 5th century BCE.[1] According to Buddhist texts, Siddhattha Gotama,[2] who later came to be known as the Buddha ("The Awakened One"), was born as a prince in the town of Lumbini (in what is today southern Nepal). His father, Suddhodana, was king of Kapilavastu, a city in today's northern India. According to the legends about the life of the Buddha, his mother, Queen Māyā, had a dream about a white elephant touching her side. This dream was interpreted by the wise men at the court to mean that she was pregnant and would give birth to a son. But this son, it was predicted, was either going to be the greatest ruler the world had ever seen, or the greatest renouncer. To make sure that he became a great king, rather than a renouncer, his father kept him sheltered from the suffering of the world outside the palace. Although he was raised in luxury inside a royal palace, away from all suffering, prince Siddhattha longed to know more about life outside the palace walls.

Siddhattha married his cousin Yasodharā, and they had a son, Rahūla, but the young father was still not happy. Sneaking out of the palace accompanied by his servant, Siddhattha eventually saw four things that would change the course of his life forever ("The four signs"): an old man, a sick man, a dead body, and a wandering ascetic. For the first time in his life, the spoiled prince was confronted with the reality of old age, disease, and death, and he realized the

[1] The precise dates of the life of Siddhattha Gotama are debated. The Ceylonese Long Chronology based on chronicles from Sri Lanka dates the life of the Buddha from 624 to 544 BCE. The Corrected Long Chronology uses the dates 567–487 BCE, while the Indian Short Chronology based on Indian sources as well as Tibetan and Chinese translations uses the dates 448–368 BCE. The Modern Chronology has adjusted the dates of the Buddha to 563–483 BCE. The chronicles from Sri Lanka state that the Buddha died 218 years before the consecration of the emperor Aśoka, which they date to 326 BCE. The Corrected Long Chronology accepts that 218 years passed between the death of the Buddha and the consecration of Aśoka, but dates the consecration to 268 BCE. The Indian Short Chronology is based on Vinaya (monastic discipline) texts that place the Buddhist Council of Vaiśālī as well as Aśoka's consecration a mere 100 or 110 years after the Buddha's death. The Modern Chronology, accepted by many (but not all) modern scholars of Buddhism, is based on a slight adjustment of the Corrected Long Chronology and considers that sources that suggest that three years passed between Aśoka's ascent to power and his consecration ceremony. For further discussion, see Bechert 1992.

[2] Siddhattha Gotama is the Pāli version of his name, while Siddhārtha Gautama is the Sanskrit form. Sanskrit is the oldest attested language of India, and the sacred language of the Hindu scriptures. The oldest Buddhist texts are composed in the vernacular language Pāli, which was understood over large parts of North India. It is likely that the Buddha deliberately chose to give his sermons in a language that regular people could understand, rather than in Sanskrit, which would only have been understood by the learned elite. In this Element, Pāli forms will be used when discussing concepts from the Pāli canon of Theravāda Buddhism, and Sanskrit forms will be used when discussing Mahāyāna Buddhism.

impermanence of all things. But when he saw an expression of great happiness on the face of the ascetic, he decided to discover for himself what possible source of joy there could be in a world so marred by suffering. At age twenty-nine, he left his royal life and his family behind and became a wandering ascetic to discover the meaning of life. He eventually reached enlightenment while meditating under the tree that came to be known as the *bodhi* ("enlightenment") tree, and from then on, he became known as "the Buddha". Other names given to him in the Buddhist tradition are Sakyamuni ("The Sage of the Sakya Clan") and Tathāgata ("The One Who Has Gone Thus").[3] The Buddha spent the rest of his life wandering around Northern India and sharing his ideas with the people he met. He distilled his main teachings into four simple theses, which he called "The Four Noble Truths":

(1) All this is dissatisfaction (*dukkha,* Sanskrit *duḥkha*).[4]
(2) The root of dissatisfaction is desire (*taṇhā*, Sanskrit *tṛṣṇā*).
(3) Dissatisfaction is extinguished when desire is extinguished.
(4) This is accomplished by following the eightfold path.

The eightfold path to the extinction of dissatisfaction includes right understanding (*sammā diṭṭhi*), right thought (*sammā saṅkappa*), right speech (*sammā vācā*), right action (*sammā kammanta*), right livelihood (*sammā ājīva*), right effort (*sammā vāyāma*), right mindfulness (*sammā sati*), and right concentration (*sammā samādhi*). Right understanding involves understanding the four noble truths, while right thought implies detachment from desires and loving compassion toward all living beings. Right speech encompasses abstaining from lying, harsh language, divisive speech, and idle chatter, while right action is defined as abstaining from killing, stealing, and illegitimate sexual acts. Right livelihood means making one's living in a way that does not harm others. Right effort, mindfulness, and concentration, the last three stages of the eightfold path, are progressive stages of mental focus. Right effort is defined as restraining the senses and preventing unwholesome mental states from arising, while creating wholesome mental states. Right mindfulness involves a further weakening of unwholesome mental states and an unwavering focus, while right concentration is a state of complete absorption accompanied by a perfect awareness of reality.

---

[3] *Tathāgata* means either "one who has gone (*gata*) thus (*tathā*)" or "one who has come (*āgata*) thus (*tathā*)." *Tathā* ("thus") is also a term used to characterize the ultimate reality, and *Tathāgata* can also be interpreted as "one who has arrived at reality as it truly is."

[4] *Dukkha* is often translated as "suffering," but this translation is somewhat misleading. *Dukkha* is not just acute suffering and misery, but generally everything that makes a person less than satisfied with life.

How can a man who grew up in a palace claim that "all this is dissatisfaction"? Isn't this an overly pessimistic assessment of human life, which for most people contains both joy and suffering? The first noble truth should not be interpreted to mean that there is no joy in life; rather it means that all joy in *this* life is fleeting and ultimately nonsatisfactory because it is built on things that are not eternal. Human beings do not live forever; they will eventually get old and die. Youth does not last, life does not last, and any joy that is built on attachments to fleeting things will eventually be supplanted by grief. The reason why the loss of nonpermanent things leads to pain and dissatisfaction is, as the second noble truth suggests, that we are too attached to things that cannot last. The way to end dissatisfaction, then, is to free ourselves from attachments and desires. The eightfold path is meant to be a training program to achieve this.

An essential part of this eightfold path, right understanding, is grasping the impermanence of all things: everything that exists will eventually cease to exist. According to the Buddha's teachings as presented in the Pāli Canon, there is nothing eternal in this world, and therefore also no such thing as an eternal self or soul (*attā*). This lack of self is immensely difficult for humans to accept; we yearn for eternity and permanence and delude ourselves into thinking that we have an eternal soul, but this delusion is ultimately just another cause of dissatisfaction. Freedom from dissatisfaction can only be reached once humans realize that all things are fleeting and without any eternal substance. Right understanding also involves understanding the principles of *kamma* (Sanskrit *karma*) and reincarnation. The law of *kamma* (literally "action") is a moral causality inherent in the world, which means that when someone acts in a kind and helpful manner, good things will happen to them, and when someone acts in a selfish or cruel manner, bad things will come to them as a result. This is not a system of reward or punishment doled out by a divine being, but rather a universal law believed to be operating throughout the cosmos. A person's *kamma*, good or bad, will not only determine what happens to them later in this life, but also influence what sort of rebirth they will have in their next life. Many Buddhist texts postulate that there are six (sometimes five) different realms into which living beings are born: Gods (*devas*), demi-gods (*asuras*),[5] humans, animals, hungry ghosts (*peta*, Sanskrit *preta*), and hell-beings. It should be noted that while several Buddhist texts describe hellish realms, hells are merely impermanent states of terrible suffering in Buddhism, brought about by bad *kamma,* rather than any form of eternal damnation. Neither the heavens of the

[5] In the earliest Brahmanical texts of India, the Vedas, the *asuras* and the *devas* are two different types of gods. In later Hinduism, the *asuras* become demons. In Buddhist texts, *asuras* can also be viewed negatively, but not to the same extent as in classical Hinduism. The realm of the *asuras* is not always included in Buddhist lists of possible forms of rebirth.

gods nor the hells of the hell-beings are permanent in Buddhism. While gods certainly live a more luxurious existence than humans, it is nevertheless considered especially fortunate to be born a human being. Gods have it too easy and may not be sufficiently motivated to seek liberation from the cycle of death and rebirth quite yet, while animals, hungry ghosts, and hell-beings suffer too much to be able to focus on the path to enlightenment. Human life, however, contains just the optimal amount of suffering to motivate us to seek liberation.

The four noble truths are not articles of faith in Buddhism, but, rather, from the Buddhist perspective, a prescription to cure the suffering of the world. The four noble truth schema is based on the ancient Indian method for medical diagnosis: (1) What is the patient's symptoms? (2) What is the cause of the symptoms? (3) What can cure the symptom? (4) What is the doctor's prescription? In this case, the disease is the dissatisfaction inherent in human existence, and the prescription is the eightfold path that leads to *nibbāna* (Sanskrit *nirvāṇa*), a state where all dissatisfaction has ceased. How did this dissatisfaction arise in the first place? This is not an issue that is of great concern to the Buddhist texts. The Buddha addresses the irrelevance of this question with a touch of humor:

> Imagine that a man was wounded with an arrow smeared with poison. His friends and companions and relatives would bring him a doctor, but the man would say "I won't have this arrow taken out until I know whether the man who shot me was a warrior, a priest, a merchant, or a servant." He would say, "I won't have this arrow taken until I know the first and last name of the man who shot me, whether he was tall, medium, or short, whether his skin was dark, reddish brown, or golden, until I know the village, town, or city he was from, and whether the bow he shot me with was a long bow or a short one, whether the bowstring was made of plant fiber, bamboo threads, sinew, hemp, or bark, whether the bow shaft was from wild or cultivated wood, whether the feathers of the shaft came from a vulture, a stork, a hawk, a peacock, or different bird, whether it was bound with the sinew of an ox, a water buffalo, a langur, or a monkey." He would say, "I won't have this arrow taken out until I know whether it was a regular arrow, a curved arrow, a barbed arrow, a toothed arrow, or an oleander arrow." That man would die, and he still wouldn't know those things.[6]

When a person is struck by an arrow, the Buddha suggests, the important thing is to remove the arrow and alleviate his suffering, rather than worry about where exactly the arrow came from. By implication, then, the important question in Buddhism is not where suffering comes from in the first place, but what we can do to stop it.

[6] From the *Cūḷamāluṅkyovāda Sutta*, *Majjhima Nikāya* 63. Text from Trenckner 1979 (1888), I, 429–430.

Buddhism shares many main ideas with Hinduism, such as the concepts of *kamma* (*karma*) and reincarnation and the goal of escaping the endless cycle of death and rebirth. But while the post-Vedic Brahmanical tradition insists that there exists an eternal soul or self (*ātman*) in all living beings, an indestructible essence that will survive from one reincarnation to another and ultimately reach eternal union with the divine, Buddhism regards the idea of an eternal self as wishful thinking. There is *nothing* eternal, insists Buddhism – not the self, and not even gods. While Buddhist texts often feature Hindu gods, these deities are just minor characters who are neither eternal nor all-knowing.

What Is a Human Being in Buddhism?

But if there is no eternal self in Buddhism, what is a human being? Buddhism teaches that all things, including humans, are made up of psycho-physical atoms (*dhammas*, Sanskrit *dharmas*); physical objects are made up of physical atoms, while mental aspects of our existence are constructed of mental atoms. These atoms cluster together into temporary constructions. A human being is in its totality made up of five such clusters or aggregates (Pāli *khandhas,* Sanskrit: *skandhas*) of *dhammas*: physical form (*rūpa*), sensation (*vedanā*), perceptions (*saññā,* Sanskrit *saṃjñā*), mental formations (*saṅkhāra,* Sanskrit *saṃskāra)* and consciousness (*viññāna*, Sanskrit *vijñāna*). The aggregate of physical form includes the five elements (earth, water, fire, air, and ether) as well as the six sense organs (eye, ear, nose, tongue, body, and mind) and their objects (visible form, sound, smell, taste, things that can be touched, and things that can be thought). Sensations are classified as pleasant, unpleasant, and neutral feelings that arise through contact with sense-objects. There are six kinds of perceptions, corresponding to the six sense organs of eye, ear, nose, tongue, body, and mind. We should note that mind is regarded as one of the sense organs, capable of producing mental perceptions in the same way that the eye produces perceptions of visible things. Mental formations are psychological imprints are left behind by any voluntary actions humans do, which again create dispositions to act in certain ways in the future. In other words, these mental formations are habits or tendencies formed by our past actions. Consciousness is the response to the perception of an external object through one of the sense organs. Thus, when the eyes see a visible object, a visual consciousness is formed, and when the mind perceives a mental object, a mental consciousness is created, and so forth. Consciousness must not be confused with an eternal self, however; consciousness is merely a temporary formation which may last through several reincarnations but will eventually be dissolved.

The five aggregates are all marked by impermanence. The physical form that constitutes a body will be dissolved into its constituent parts when a person dies, and while the other *dhammas* may continue to hold together as aggregates through several reincarnations and attach themselves to a series of other physical forms, they too will eventually be dissolved into *dhammas* after a person reaches enlightenment.

This enlightenment is known as *nibbāna* or *nirvāṇa* in Buddhism. The term literally means "blowing out," or "extinction," as in the extinction of a flame. *Nibbāna* is extinction of all dissatisfaction and suffering and freedom from the cycle of death and rebirth. But if there is no self in Buddhism, who or what is it that reaches this state? The answer is: nobody. The person who reaches this insight was simply a construct, a conglomerate of *dhammas* that can finally dissolve. And yet this final dissolution is not perceived as nothingness in Buddhism, but rather as the ultimate bliss, a joy greater than any that is filtered through the experiences of the false ego.

The Buddha

What role does the Buddha play in helping humans reach the goal of *nibbāna*? In Theravāda Buddhism, the tradition based on the text collection called the Pāli Canon or the *Tipiṭaka*, the Buddha is primarily a teacher. Born human, he never attains any sort of divine status, although he does perform supernatural feats and miracles. Most importantly, he does attain enlightenment, and that is the most extraordinary thing of all. But although Siddhattha Gotama is often referred to as the "founder" of Buddhism, he is not regarded as unique in the Buddhist tradition. He is a Buddha by means of his extraordinary insight, but anyone who reaches the same insight on their own will also become a buddha. In the Buddhist universe, there is not just one Buddha, but countless buddhas, all defined by their ability to find release from the cycle of death and rebirth. The Pāli canon does not suggest that the Buddha should be worshipped; he is a man, not a god, and he is dead, not still living. But his teachings, his *dhamma*, remains in the world as a source of inspiration for those who similarly wish to follow the eightfold path to enlightenment and freedom from dissatisfaction.

Theravāda and Mahāyāna Buddhism

After the first few centuries of Buddhist history, the Buddhist community split into several branches. Today, the two main forms of Buddhism are Theravāda ("The Doctrine of the Elders") and Mahāyāna ("The Great Vehicle"). Theravāda Buddhism is primarily found in South and Southeast Asia (Sri Lanka, Thailand, Myanmar, Cambodia, and Laos), while Mahāyāna Buddhism is found in Tibet,

China, Mongolia, Vietnam, Korea, and Japan. An offshoot of Mahāyāna, Vajrayāna ("The Thunderbolt Vehicle") is sometimes regarded as a separate branch of Buddhism. This branch, often associated with Tibetan culture, is found in Tibet, Nepal, Bhutan, and Mongolia.

Theravāda Buddhism still uses the language of the oldest Buddhist scriptures, Pāli, a simple vernacular language assumed to have been used by the Buddha to communicate to regular people in the 5th century BCE, as a sacred language. Mahāyāna Buddhist scriptures, on the other hand, are composed in India's ancient culture language Sanskrit, the sacred language of Hinduism, as well as in regional languages like Tibetan, Chinese, and Japanese. Another essential distinction between the two branches of Buddhism lies in how they view the Buddha and other enlightened beings. In Theravāda Buddhism, the ideal figure is an *arahat*, a human monk who has devoted himself to the eightfold path and works diligently through meditation to reach *nibbāna*. In Mahāyāna Buddhism, on the other hand, the ideal figure is a *bodhisattva* (Sanskrit: "one whose very being (*sattva*) is enlightenment (*bodhi*)"). A bodhisattva is a being (often human, but not always) who has reached enlightenment, but chooses to step back on the very brink of *nirvāṇa* and return to the cycle of death and rebirth to assist suffering beings in reaching enlightenment as well. A bodhisattva is not reborn because of *karma* like humans, animals, or even gods are, but rather voluntarily and out of their great compassion. A bodhisattva will take on any form – human, animal, or other – and work tirelessly for the benefit of all living beings. As we will discuss in a later section, although they are not regarded as gods, bodhisattvas can become something akin to savior figures in Mahāyāna Buddhism.

Buddhist Canons

As Lewis Lancaster has observed, the term "Buddhist canon" is something of a misnomer; instead of a single authoritative collection of sacred texts, Buddhism has a veritable library of such collections: the Pāli canon of Theravāda Buddhism, the Sanskrit *Mahāyāna Sūtras*, the Chinese Buddhist canon, the Tibetan Kanjur (*bka'-'gyur*) and Tenjur (*bstan-'gyur*), the Korean *Tripiṭaka*, the Mongolian Buddhist canon, the Manchu Buddhist canon, the Tangut Buddhist canon, and so on, preserved in tens of thousands of manuscripts in different scripts and languages.[7]

The Pāli Canon is the primary scripture collection of Theravāda Buddhism, the oldest surviving Buddhist school. It is composed in Pāli, a Middle Indic language derived from Sanskrit and is also known as the *Tipiṭaka* ("Three

[7] Lancaster 1979, 215.

Baskets"), perhaps because the texts were once stored in three separate baskets. The *Tipiṭaka* is divided into three sections: (1) The *Vinaya Piṭaka* ("The Basket of Discipline"), which contains rules and regulations for monastic life; (2) The *Sutta Piṭaka* ("The Basket of Discourses") consisting of teachings attributed to the Buddha, including discourses on ethics, meditation, and wisdom; and (3) The *Abhidhamma Piṭaka* ("The Basket of Things Relating to the Teachings"), which presents systematic philosophical analyses of Buddhist doctrines.

According to the Theravāda Buddhist tradition, the *Sutta Piṭaka*, which purports to contain the words of the Buddha, was recited orally by the disciple Ānanda at the First Buddhist Council held after the Buddha's death. Another disciple, Upāli, recited the *Vinaya Piṭaka.* After that, these texts came to be regarded as authoritative, transmitted orally and eventually written down along with the *Abhidhamma Piṭaka* during the Fourth Buddhist Council, which took place some 450 years after the death of the Buddha. But the establishment of the canon was not completely without controversy; the Theravāda texts tell of one monk, Purāṇa, who was late for the first council and refused to accept the version of the text accepted by those present because it was different from the way he had heard it from the Buddha.

But there are also other Buddhist canons. The Mahāyāna Sūtras are a vast collection of scriptures that form the basis of Mahāyāna Buddhism. These texts include discourses attributed to the Buddha as well as teachings attributed to various bodhisattvas. The Mahāyāna Sūtras emphasize the ideal of the bodhisattva, who seeks enlightenment not only for their own liberation but also for the benefit of all sentient beings. Some of the most well-known Mahāyāna Sūtras include the *Heart Sūtra*, the *Lotus Sūtra*, and the *Diamond Sūtra*.

The Chinese Tripiṭaka is a vast collection of Buddhist scriptures and texts that were translated into Chinese over many centuries. Like the Pāli canon, it is divided into a *Vinaya Piṭaka*, a *Sutta Piṭaka*, and an *Abhidhamma Piṭaka*. Texts translated from both Pāli and Sanskrit are included, as well as some texts that do not have Indian exemplars. The Chinese Tripiṭaka played a crucial role in the spread and development of Buddhism in East Asia, including China, Korea, Japan, and Vietnam. It provided the foundation for the establishment of Buddhist monastic institutions, the training of monks and nuns, and the dissemination of Buddhist teachings to a wider audience.

The Tibetan Buddhist canon consists of two separate collections of scriptures, the *Kanjur* (Tibetan *bka'-'gyur*, "translation of the word") and the *Tanjur* (Tibetan *bstan-'gyur,* "translation of treatises"). The Kanjur is a collection of scriptures that contain teachings attributed to the Buddha. It consists of approximately 100 volumes of the translated words of the Buddha as well as commentaries by Indian Buddhist scholars. The texts cover a wide range of topics including ethics, philosophy, meditation, and rituals. Like the *Tipiṭaka*, the *Kanjur* is divided into three main sections: *Vinaya*, *sutta*, and *abhidhamma*. The *Tanjur* is a collection of commentaries and treatises written by Indian Buddhist masters and scholars. It serves as a complement to the *Kanjur*, providing explanations, interpretations, and analyses of the Buddha's teachings found in the *Kanjur*. The *Tanjur* consists of around 225 volumes and covers a vast array of subjects including philosophy, logic, psychology, and metaphysics.

Buddhism – an Atheistic Religion?

Several scholars have argued that Buddhism can be seen as an atheistic religion.[8] But what does this mean? The concept of an atheistic religion may seem paradoxical at first glance. For many people, atheism seems to be the very opposite of religion, which by many common definitions would include the belief in a higher being or beings.

Atheism has been defined in several different ways. Baggini, for example, defines atheism as "the belief that there is no God or gods."[9] But Baggini also adds: "The atheist's rejection of belief in God is usually accompanied by a broader rejection of any supernatural or transcendental reality."[10] Bullivant and Ruse define atheism as "the absence of belief in a God or gods," while Cliteur claims that "an atheist does not believe in the god that theism favors."[11] At first sight, it may seem that these definitions say almost the same thing, but on closer inspection, there are some significant differences between them. To believe, emphatically, that there is no God or gods is different from just not having a belief in a God or gods"; in the latter case, people may not absolutely rule out the existence of gods, even though they do not themselves believe in the existence of deities.[12] Cliteur's definition adds another level of complexity to the definition of atheism; by his definition, atheism is not the lack of belief in gods per se, but rather the lack of belief in the specific concept of God/gods found in theism, that is, a God or gods believed to have created the world, who rule over the world and the living beings in it, and who lead humans to salvation.

By these definitions, would Buddhism be a form of atheism? That depends. Many Buddhists do believe in the existence of gods, but these gods are merely superhuman entities that did not create the world, do not rule over it, and play no role in the human path to salvation. In other words, while Buddhists may believe in gods, these are not the gods that "theism favors." The *devas* (gods) of

[8] See for example Bullivant (2013, 15). [9] Baggini 2003, 3. [10] Baggini 2003, 3.

[11] Bullivant and Ruse 2013, 2; Cliteur 2009, 1.

[12] The first type is often referred to as "positive atheism," while the second is referred to as "negative atheism." See Martin 2007, 1; Bullivant 2013, 15.

Buddhism are super-human, but they are not eternal, all-knowing, or all-powerful. Chemparathy writes that Buddhists view gods "merely as beings of a superior order with a life longer than that of ordinary mortals and enjoying great happiness."[13]

Buddhism is atheistic in that it denies the existence of an eternal all-powerful God, but it is not a pure materialism that denies the existence of any spiritual reality beyond the world of the senses.[14] As von Glasenapp has noted, some scholars have still tried in various way to present the case that Buddhism is still a theistic religion, mostly by arguing that the Buddha did not deny the existence of gods, or that an abstract concept such as *nibbāna* takes on the role of a God, or that the Buddha was regarded as a God by his followers.[15] It is nevertheless clear that the oldest Buddhist texts are functionally atheistic, even though the existence of gods is never denied. Buddhism operates with the idea that nothing is permanent, and that also includes the *devas*. The *devas* are more than humans, but they are also much less than the gods of theistic religions who are creators and rulers of the world and redeemers of a suffering humanity. In Buddhism, any human being can become a *deva* due to accumulation of good *kamma*, but they will be reborn as something else once that *kamma* has been used up.

When Buddhism is referred to as "atheistic," this does not mean that there are no gods in Buddhism. On the contrary, the Buddhist texts mention many gods – gods who bow down to the Buddha, argue with him, or encourage him to spread his teachings – and shrines to deities are often found alongside Buddha images in Buddhist communities around the world. But these Buddhist gods are nevertheless peripheral to the Buddhist teachings. They play no role in creating the world or in bringing human beings to salvation. Although they have powers and lifespans that exceed those of humans, they are neither all-powerful nor eternal. Buddhism depicts gods as supernatural beings that are completely irrelevant to human salvation, mere interesting and interested spectators and to the cosmic drama of suffering, rebirth, and liberation. The Buddha did not deny the existence of deities (*devas*). He did, however, categorically deny that the world is created by a god, or that gods are eternal.

In Buddhism, there is no divine creator and no divine ruler of the world. Where, then, did the world come from? The Buddhist texts hint that the world was probably always here, but more significantly, they regard the question of the world's origin as rather uninteresting. No matter where it came from, the world *is* here, and it is filled with suffering, a suffering that urgently needs to be alleviated. And that suffering is not something that the *devas* can do much about.

---

[13] Chemparathy 1968–69, 85. [14] Nyanaponika 1960, v. [15] Von Glasenapp 1966, 42.

When asked directly by his Brahman student whether gods exist, the Buddha gives an answer that at first sight seems rather vague and evasive:

> "How is it, venerable Gotama, are there gods?" "It is known to me, Bhāradvāja, that there are gods." "How is it, venerable Gotama, that when asked 'Are there gods?' you say: 'It is known to me, Bhāradvāja, that there are gods.' If that is so, isn't what you say empty and untrue?' "'Bhāradvāja, when asked, 'Are there gods?' whether I answer, 'There are gods,' or 'It is known to me that there are gods,' a wise man may conclude that there are gods." "But why didn't the venerable Gotama give me the first answer?" "It is commonly accepted in the world, Bhāradvāja, that there are gods."[16]

The Buddha's answer certainly confirms that gods exist, but the answer comes across as more of a bored "Yes, everyone knows that" rather than a positive affirmation of their essence. Perhaps the Buddha's tone is meant to convey that while it is known that gods exist, their existence is not all that relevant or exciting. The Buddha is not telling his followers not to worship gods, however. On another occasion, the Buddha tells two of his followers:

> Wherever a wise man lives, there he brings offerings to the gods that dwell there. He respects and reveres the gods, and they respect and revere him. They tremble for him, as a mother trembles for her son.[17]

Here, the Buddha seems to suggest that it may be a good idea to venerate local deities and establish a mutually beneficial relationship with them. These deities are then able to watch over and protect a person. What these *devas* cannot do, as we will see in other Buddhist texts, is take any part in a person's salvation or bring any deeper meaning to their lives. They are more like supernatural helpers that can do a person little favors.

The *Tevijja Sutta,* a text of the Pāli Canon, contains a pointed critique of Hindu Brahmans (priests) who claim to know an eternal god.[18] Two Brahmans, Vāseṭṭha and Bhāradvāja, argue about how to obtain union with the divine creator Brahmā. Brahmā is described in this text as the one who has mastery that others do not have mastery over (*abhibhū anabhibhūto*), lord (*issaro*), and creator (*kattā*). The two Brahmans go to the Buddha and asks him how to obtain Brahmā. The Buddha asks them if they know anyone who has ever met Brahmā, and when it turns out that they don't, the Buddha tells them that their goal of obtaining union with someone no one has ever met is completely pointless:

---

16 From the *Saṅgārava Sutta*, *Majjhima Nikāya* 100, 42. Text from Chalmers 1977 (1896), 212–213.

17 *Mahāparinibbāna Sutta, Dīgha Nikāya* 16.1.31. Text from Rhys Davids and Carpenter 1966 (1903), 88–89.

18 *Tevijja Sutta. Dīgha Nikāya* 13. Text from Rhys Davids and Carpenter 1975 (1890), 235–253.

> The Brahmans themselves admit that nobody has seen Brahmā with their own eyes. So they actually teach: "We show you the way to someone we don't know and don't see, and this way is the only way to reach him." This is as if one wanted to build a staircase to the upper floor of a palace one has never seen and whose size one doesn't know. Or it is as if a person said: "I love the most beautiful woman in a particular country and I want to marry her", but doesn't know when asked for her name, her appearance, her house, or her dwelling place. Isn't this vain and foolish talk?[19]

There is a strong element of critique of the Hindu worship of deities here, and a suggestion that sacrifices to the gods are meaningless. The Buddha does not tell the two Brahmans that the creator god Brahmā does not exist, but rather that there is no evidence whatsoever that he does, and that it is therefore meaningless to pursue union someone who might not even exist. This passage suggests that the gods are nothing more than human fantasies, based on no experiential evidence at all, and traditional religion just a "staircase to nowhere."

The Mahāyāna Buddhist philosopher Nāgārjuna put it even more pointedly:

> The gods are all eternal scoundrels,
> Incapable of dissolving the suffering of impermanence.
> Those who serve them and venerate them
> may even in this world sink into a sea of sorrow.
> Those who despise them and blaspheme
> may in this world know all kinds of fortune.
> We know the gods are false and have no concrete being;
> therefore the wise man believes them not.
> The fate of the world depends on causes and conditions;
> therefore the wise man does not rely on gods.[20]

But insisting that one should not rely on gods does not imply that they do not exist. As the *Aṅguttara Nikāya* states:

> As far and suns and moons extend their paths and the regions of the sky light up with splendor, there are a thousand worlds. In each one of these worlds there are a thousand suns, moons, Meru mountains, four thousand continents and oceans, a thousand heavens and realms of sensory pleasures, and a thousand worlds of Brahmā. As far as the thousand worlds reach, the great Brahmā is the highest being. But even the great Brahmā comes into being and then ceases to be.[21]

Brahmā is a creator god in Hinduism, and he is described in positive terms in several Buddhist texts. But even Brahmā is ultimately part of the cycle of death

---

19 *Poṭṭhapāda Sutta, Dīgha Nikāya* 9.35. Text from Rhys Davids and Carpenter 1975 (1890), 193.
20 *Mahāprajñāpāramitāśāstra*, text from Lamotte 1944, 141.
21 *Paṭhamakosalasutta, Anguttara Nikāya* 10.29.2, text from Hardy 1900 (1958), 59.

and rebirth, as mortal as human beings are. The path to salvation, therefore, does not lie in the worship of deities in Buddhism, but rather in the following of the eightfold path. The Buddha, significantly, is called "the teacher of gods and humans," which suggests that gods themselves are beings in need of instruction and liberation in Buddhism, just as humans are.

Can Buddhism, then, be defined as an atheistic? That depends on our definition of atheism. Buddhism does not deny the existence of the minor deities called *devas,* and these gods and goddesses are occasionally worshipped, as we shall see, in popular Buddhism. But Buddhism does emphatically and repeatedly refute the existence of an *Īśvara*, a god who creates the world, rules over it, and holds humans accountable.

While some scholars have argued that "atheism" is a modern and Western construct, and that applying the term to pre-modern and non-Western cultures is both anachronistic and a form of "epistemic violence" (Spivak 1999, 205) or "mental colonialism" (Quack 2016, 652), one could also argue that our modern and Western understanding of atheism as a heuristic category is greatly enriched and expanded by being challenged by Buddhist sources. While we cannot equate forms of modern Western "atheism" with the modes of thought found in ancient India, studying the multiple strands of Buddhist thought from ancient South Asia that reject the concept of a personal god helps us think about the usefulness of "atheism" as an analytical category in new and interesting ways. Buddhism is strongly anti-theistic but postulates the existence of both minor deities (*devas*) and of a sacred reality beyond the confines of the material world.

2 Buddhism and the Idea of a Divine Creator

Where did the world come from? Was it created by a divine being, or did it somehow come into existence on its own? Or has the world always been here? These are questions that have occupied many ancient Indian philosophers. While Hindu mythology is rich in stories about creator gods, Buddhist philosophers argue that the idea of a divine creator of the universe is logically untenable. This section outlines some Buddhist ideas of causality and discusses the arguments against the existence of a divine Prime Mover or creator god.

Buddhist Causality

Buddhist philosophers observe that the world is governed by laws of cause and effect. All phenomena in this world, whether physical or mental, appear to have a cause. Plants grow from seeds, animals and humans are born from their parents, and actions – whether good, bad, or neutral – have consequences. Like Hinduism and Jainism, Buddhism teaches a doctrine of *kamma*

(Sanskrit: *karma*), the idea that all intentional actions a person performs will lead to positive or negative effects on that person's life in the future, or even on their future lives. These positive or negative consequences of human actions are part of a natural law of causality that governs the world.

Causality is central to the Buddha's teachings. The Buddha declared that the doctrine of dependent origination (Pāli *paṭiccasamuppāda*, Sanskrit *pratītyasamutpāda*) was key to understanding his teachings: "Those who perceive dependent origination will perceive the *dhamma* [teaching]; those who perceive the *dhamma* will perceive dependent origination."[22] Simply put, dependent origination is the idea that all phenomena in the world arise from other phenomena. Nothing exists independently of a cause; nothing has any sort of eternal existence of its own. This idea is in direct contradiction to Hindu philosophy which does operate with eternal, uncaused principles, such as the divine force of *brahman* or the eternal soul *ātman*.

One of the texts of the Pāli canon, the *Saṃyutta Nikāya*, summarizes the Buddhist view of causation:

> When x exists, y comes to be. With the arising (*uppāda*) of x, y arises. When x does not exist, then y does not come to be. With the cessation (*nirodha*) of x, y ceases.[23]

This type of causation is clearly seen in the four noble truths of Buddhism (see Section 1). Dissatisfaction is not without a cause; it is brought about by desire. Once that cause is eliminated, dissatisfaction itself will cease. The idea of dependent origination in Buddhism is often summarized in a list of twelve causal factors (*nidānas*):

1) Ignorance (*avijjā*)
2) Mental formations (*saṃkhāra*)
3) Consciousness (*viññāna*)
4) Name and form (*nāmarūpa*)
5) The six senses (*saḷāyatana*)
6) Touch (*phassa*)
7) Sensation (*vedanā*)
8) Desire (*taṇhā*)
9) Attachment (*upādāna*)
10) Existence (*bhava*)
11) Birth (*jāti*)
12) Old age and death (*jāramaraṇa*)

---

[22] *Vakkali, Saṃyutta Nikāya* 22. 87.13. Text from Feer 1890 (1975), 120.

[23] *Assutavato, Saṃyutta Nikāya* 12.61.9. Text from Feer 1888 (1970), 95.

All existence as we know it, including birth, old age, and death, is caused by something, and the doctrine of dependent origination claims that the ultimate cause is our own ignorance. The good news is that this ignorance can be removed, which will also result in the cessation of desire, birth, old age, and death. Dependent origination, not a divine creator, explains how our world came to be in Buddhism. But where did the first part of this causal chain, ignorance, come from in the first place? Buddhism provides no answer to that question; it merely provides a remedy for that ignorance.

The Refutation of the Idea of Creator

While many religious traditions turn to the idea of a divine creator as the first cause of all things that exist, Buddhist philosophers go to great lengths to refute such an idea. If God created to universe, so the Buddhist argument goes, then who created God? The idea of an eternal God who is the first cause of all things goes against the grain of Buddhism, which is a tradition that emphasizes the impermanence of all things. All things, argue the Buddhists, come into being because something caused them to be; there is nothing and nobody in the world that is eternally existent. According to Buddhist thought, the doctrine of *kamma,* which implies a causal cycle without beginning and end, is not compatible with the idea of a creator as first cause. If there was a creator and a beginning of time, how could the cycle of action and consequences even begin, since every *kammic* result is caused by a previous action?

Hindu texts often refer to an *Īśvara* ("lord") as the creator and ruler of the world, a divine figure often identified with gods like Brahmā, Viṣṇu, or Śiva. Buddhist texts repeatedly refute the idea of an *Īśvara* (Pāli *Issara*) as the creator and ruler of the world. In the *Brahmajāla Sutta,* the very first text of the *Dīgha Nikāya* ("Collection of Long Discourses"), the Buddha explains sixty-two erroneous views which will hinder a person from reaching enlightenment. One of these views is the idea that the world is created by a God. This erroneous view is not only held by humans, according to this text, but by the gods themselves, including the Hindu creator god Brahmā:

> There comes a time, brothers, after a long period of time, when this world system passes away. When this happens, beings will have been reborn in a world of radiance, where they will live, consisting of mind, feeding on joy, radiating light, travelling through the air, and dwelling in glory. They remain like this for a long time.
>
> Then there comes a time, brothers, when this world system evolves again. When this happens, the Palace of Brahmā appears, but it is empty. Then some being falls from the world of radiance, either because his lifespan is used up or because his merit is exhausted, and he is born into the Palace of Brahmā.

> There he lives consisting of mind, feeding on joy, radiating light, travelling through the air, and dwelling in glory. He lives there for a long time.
>
> Since he lives there so long by himself, a longing arises in him. "I wish that other beings might come and join me in this place." And then other beings fall from the world of radiance, either because their lifespans are used up of because their merit is exhausted, and they appear in the Palace of Brahmā as companions to him, seemingly like him.
>
> Now, brothers, the one who was first reborn there thinks to himself: "I am Brahmā, the great Brahmā, the mighty, all-seeing one, the ruler, the lord of all, the maker, the creator, the king of all, which has put each one in his place, the ancient one, the father of all that is and all that will be. These other beings are my creation. Why is that the case? Because I thought a while ago "I wish that they might come", and the beings came as a result of my mental wish."
>
> And those beings also think thus: "He must be Brahmā, the great, the mighty, all-seeing one, the ruler, the lord of all, the maker, the creator, the king of all, which has put each one in his place, the ancient one, the father of all that is and all that will be. And we must have been created by him, because he was here first, and we came after that."[24]

In this text, the god Brahmā himself and the other gods are under the illusion that Brahmā is the creator of the world and of the other gods, just because he happened to be the first to be reincarnated in the "Palace of Brahmā." In reality, according to this text, Brahmā is no creator, but rather himself a being who undergoes reincarnation due to *kamma*.

There are also texts dealing with the question of a creator god in the *Majjhima Nikāya* ("Middle-Length Discourses") of the *Sutta Piṭaka*. The *Devadaha-sutta* uses the argument of human suffering to disprove the existence of a benevolent creator god who rules over the world. Some people some claim that pleasure and pain are created by God (*Issara*). But, the text observes, if people like the ascetic Jains have to suffer through their pious austerities, then they must have been created by an evil creator rather than by a benevolent God.[25]

The same idea is found in the *Anguttara Nikāya* ("Collection of Numerical Discourses") of the *Sutta Piṭaka:*

> Some ascetics and Brahmans hold: "Whatever comes to man, happiness or dissatisfaction, or neither, all is caused by the will of the creator (*issara-nimmāna*)." [. . .] But I say: "So then because of the will of their creator and God, human beings become murderers, thieves, unchaste, liars, slanderers, covetous, malicious and heretical. And those who rely on the creation of a supreme God lack the desire and energy to do what is to be done, and to refrain from doing what is not to be done."[26]

[24] *Brahmajāla Sutta, Dīgha Nikāya* 1.2.2–1.2.5, text from Davids and Carpenter 1975, 17–18.
[25] *Devadaha-sutta* (*Majjhima Nikāya* 101), Trenckner 1888, 227.
[26] *Anguttara Nikāya* 3. 61.1. Text from Morris 1885 (1961), 173.

We also encounter similar ideas in some of the *Jātakas* ("Birth Stories"), tales of the Buddha's previous lives collected in the *Khuddaka Nikāya* ("Short Discourses") of the *Sutta Piṭaka*. The *Mahābodhijātaka* tells the story of a king who has five evil advisors, who all hold erroneous views of different kinds.

> One of them denied causality. Another believed that everything is the work of a Supreme Being. The third taught the doctrine of previous actions. The fourth believed in annihilation in death. The fifth believed in the Kṣatriya [warrior] doctrine.
>
> The one who denied causality taught that beings in the world are purified at rebirth. The one who believed in the work of a Supreme Being taught that He had created the world. The one who taught the doctrine of previous actions taught that the sorrow and joy that happens to someone here is the result of a previous action. The one who believed annihilation at death taught that no one goes from here into another world, but that this world is destroyed. He who taught the Kṣatriya doctrine taught that one should do what's in one's own best interest, even killing one's parents. These men were appointed judges in the king's court, but they were greedy and took bribes and took the property of the rightful owners.[27]

The king is, not surprisingly, led astray by these ill-informed and wicked advisors, but he is eventually taught the truth by the Buddha-to-be:

> So the Great Being [the future Buddha] criticized him and reduced him to silence. The king, feeling annoyed at being criticized before the assembly, collapsed and sat down. And the great Being, after refuting his heresy, addressed the one who believed that everything is brought about by a Supreme Being and said, "Why, sir, do you blame me, if you really fall back upon the doctrine that everything is the creation of a Supreme Being?" And he repeated this verse:
>
> If happiness and dissatisfaction, as well as the good and bad actions of the whole world are determined by the Lord, then a person just acts according to his will. By that, it is the Lord who is defiled (through bad actions).[28]

In other words, the future Buddha argues that an all-powerful and benevolent God would not have allowed evil to exist in the world, foreshadowing the classical theodicy or "problem of evil" later discussed in Europe by philosophers like Plotinus, Augustine, and Leibniz. But while Plotinus and Augustine argue that evil is merely the absence of good, and Leibniz proposes that God has created the best of all possible worlds, the Buddhist philosophers use the problem of evil to argue against the existence of God.

---

[27] *Mahābodhijātaka,* text from Fausbøll 1891, 228.

[28] *Mahābodhijātaka,* text from Fausbøll 1891, 230.

In Aśvaghoṣa's *Buddhacarita*, a 2nd-century-CE Sanskrit epic about the life of the Buddha, one of the characters says:

> Some say that creation comes from Īśvara. But if so, why does a person even need to act? That which is the cause of action in the world is also the cause of the cessation of action."[29]

The implication of this argument is that if a personal God rules over everything in the world, nothing that a person does will make a difference. This is shown to be a wrong view in this text, where a person's actions are regarded as highly efficacious. Aśvaghoṣa implies that a God who rules over the world and determines the outcome of events is a direct contradiction of the doctrine of *karma*. If God decides what will happen, there is no point to human action at all.

A similar argument is made in Buddhaghosa's 5th-century Theravāda philosophical treatise *Visuddhimagga* ("The Path of Purification"). Here, the Buddha's teaching that dissatisfaction arises from our own desires is presented as a better alternative to the idea that *Issara* created a suffering world:

> Knowledge of the origin of dissatisfaction ends any misunderstanding about causes, such as the belief that something is a cause when it is not – like the idea that the world arises because of God, primordial matter, time, or inherent qualities.[30]

Similar ideas are expressed by the great Mahāyāna philosophers of the Mādhyamaka and Yogācara schools. The founder of the Mādhyamaka school was Nāgārjuna, who lived around the 2nd to 3rd centuries CE. Nāgārjuna is particularly well known for his work *Mūlamadhyamakakārikā* ("Root Verses on the Middle Way"), where he defines the crucial concept of "emptiness" (*śūnyatā*) as *pratītyasamutpāda*, dependent origination. For Nāgārjuna, all phenomena are empty, not in the sense that they are nonexistent or illusory, but because they lack eternal "essence" (*svabhāva*). All things in this world are caused by other things, and nothing just *exists,* in and of itself. This, to Nāgārjuna, is what emptiness is, and a correct view of emptiness in integral to liberation. For Nāgārjuna, the idea of a creator God, a first uncaused cause, does not work. As we saw in the previous section, Nāgārjuna does not hesitate to mock the very idea of a divine creator or ruler of the world. Perhaps this is why a small treatise on the refutation of a creator god (*Īśvarakartṛtvanirākṛti Viṣṇorekakartṛtvanirākaraṇam*, "The Refutation of Īśvara as the Creator – The Refutation of Viṣṇu as Sole Creator") is listed among the numerous works ascribed to Nāgārjuna in the Tibetan Buddhist canon, the

[29] *Buddhacarita* 9. 53. Text from the online edition at https://ancient-buddhist-texts.net/Buddhist-Texts/S2-Buddhacarita/index.htm.

[30] Text from Rewatadhamma 1969, 1156.

Tanjur. Although it is unlikely to be a genuine composition of Nāgārjuna's, the text is interesting enough in itself:

> Moved by compassion, I write this for the instruction of good disciples after greeting the lotus feet of my teacher and Vajrasattva. [Some people argue:] There is indeed an Īśvara who is the creator; let him be considered. He who makes is a creator, and he who performs an action is called a creator.
>
> But as far as this is concerned, we say: Does he create that which already exists, or that which does not already exist? First, he does not create that which already exists, because that is not creation. Thus, when an individual (*pudgala*) exists, there is no creation by the maker who brings it into being, since it already exists.
>
> But on the other hand, if you say that he creates that which does not already exist, [we say]: Oil coming from sand does not exist, and hairs coming from a tortoise does not exist. Let Īśvara make those! But he cannot be a creator of these things. Why? Because it is in their nature that they don't exist. This is how it is.
>
> But maybe he creates that which both already exists and doesn't exist? That cannot be right because of mutual contradiction. For that which exists, does indeed exist, and that which does not exist, does not exist at all. Therefore, there would be a mutual contradiction between these two things, just like between light and darkness and between life and death. For where there is light, there is no darkness, and where there is darkness, there is no light. He who is alive is alive, and he who is dead is dead. For this same reason, because a thing cannot be existent and not existent at the same time, our view is that Īśvara cannot be the creator.
>
> There is also another objection. Does he who creates other beings himself have an origin, or did he not have an origin?
>
> He cannot create other beings without having an origin himself. Why is that? Because he himself has a nature that has no origin. Just as the son of a barren woman, who has not had an origin, cannot do anything, such as digging with a spade, and so forth, so it is also for Īśvara.
>
> But if he himself had an origin and then creates other beings, where did he have his origin? Did he originate from himself, or from another being, or both?
>
> He cannot have originated from himself because any activity directed at one's own self is contradictory. Even the blade of a very sharp sword cannot cut itself, and a young dancer, though very limber, cannot climb up on his own shoulders and dance. It is not observed, nor is it correct, that a person is both the creator and the created. It is not known in this world that a person is himself his own father and himself his own son.
>
> But if he were to come from another, that would also not be right. For as long as Īśvara does not exist, another being would not exist. Or maybe they create each other in turn. But even if he originates from another in this way, this would lead to infinite regress, since it is without beginning. The refutation of the termination of that which has no beginning is nothing but its non-existence. When a seed is absent, there is the non-existence of the sprout, trunk branches, leaves, flowers, fruits, and so on. Why? Because of the absence of the seed.

> Īśvara can also not have originated both from himself and from another since that would be contradicted by the defects mentioned above. Therefore, a creator of the universe cannot be proven.[31]

While Nāgārjuna would no doubt have agreed with this text's author that the universe is not created by a God, the prose of the brief Sanskrit text is plain and inelegant and has very little in common with Nāgārjuna's style or with the sophistication of his philosophical arguments as seen in works like his *Mūlamadhyamakārikā*. The *Īśvarakartṛtvanirākṛti* is included in the Tibetan canon in both Sanskrit and Tibetan, with a colophon listing Nāgārjuna as its author.[32] Chemparathy argues that the attribution of the text to Nāgārjuna in the colophon is wrong, since the text's opening verse mentions the bodhisattva Vajrasattva, whose cult is not attested until centuries later.[33] The full title and colophon of the text mention Viṣṇu, but the text itself does not, and the text can therefore be read as an argument against any creator god, rather than against the teachings of a particular group of Hindu devotees.[34]

The other main philosophical school of Mahāyāna Buddhism is Yogācāra (literally "The Practice of Yoga," although its teachings are different from those of the Hindu philosophical school that bears the name of Yoga). Yogācāra is also known as *Cittamātra* ("Mind Only") or *Vijñānavāda* ("The School of Consciousness"). This school was founded by Asaṅga in the 4th century CE. Asaṅga is the author of a vast compendium on Yogācāra philosophy known as the *Yogācārabhūmi* ("The Foundation of Yogācāra").[35] The *Yogācārabhūmi* lists sixteen erroneous views, which include two different arguments for the existence of God. "Everything that a human individual experiences is caused either by the activity of Īśvara or by the activity of another person," the text claims in its opening passage, before going on to refute this argument. According to the *Yogācārabhūmi*, people make this claim about the existence of Īśvara based either on sacred scriptures (*āgama*) or on logical reasoning (*yukti*). Asaṅga does not even bother to discuss the claim to scriptural authority, but he goes on to discuss the flaws in the logical argument for the existence of a creator at some length:

> [They say] "Living beings think when they cause something: 'We shall do what is good,' but also do what is bad without wanting to. And at the time of reaping the fruit of their action, they think: 'We shall be born into a good

31 Text from Thomas 1903, 345–349.

32 The text was published in Thomas 1903 and is analyzed in Chemparathy 1968–69.

33 Chemparathy 1968–69, 91.

34 Chemparathy 1968–69, 94.

35 Some scholars believe that the text was likely composed over several generations around 300–400 CE and is unlikely to be a single author's work (Chemparathy 1968–69, Frauwallner 1958, 265).

existence in the heavenly world among the gods', but instead they are born into a bad existence. Although they think, 'We will experience happiness', they experience only unhappiness. This happens to them [they assume] through someone who is the maker, the creator, the builder, the father of living beings, an Īśvara or someone else."

Such a person should be corrected as follows:

'[This cannot be the case because Īśvara] does not have the ability to create the world. There would be a contradiction because he would be both immanent and non-immanent. There would be the error that he would both have and not have a purpose for creation, as well as the fact that he would be a cause. Do you mean that his ability to create has as its cause either the performance of work or no cause at all? If it has the performance of work as its cause, then this is not right, for the universe would then have the performance of work as its cause. But if it has no cause, then it is not right (to claim a creator).

Do you mean that Īśvara is immanent or that he is not immanent? If he is immanent, then it's not right to say that he creates the world, since he would have the same nature as the world. If he is not immanent, then it's not right to say that he creates the world since he would have no relation to it'.

Do you mean that Īśvara has a purpose or does not have a purpose [in creating the world]? If he creates for a purpose, then it is not right to say that he is the lord of the world, since he would not be the lord of that purpose [that drives him to create]. And if he creates without purpose, then it's not correct to say that he both has no purpose and that he creates.

Do you mean that the creation is cause by Īśvara alone, of that it is also caused by a material cause different from him? If the world has Īśvara alone as its cause, then where there is Īśvara, there is creation, and where there is creation, there is Īśvara. Then it would not be correct to say that the creation is caused by Īśvara. If it is also caused by a material cause different from him, then is it caused by his will or some other material cause without his will? If it is caused by his will, is that will caused by Īśvara alone, or is it caused by some material cause other than him? If it is caused by Īśvara alone, when there is Īśvara, there is his will, and when there is his will, there is Īśvara, and therefore there would be creation at all times. But if it is caused by some material cause other than him, then such a cause is not observed. It is not right to say that he is the lord of the world, if he is not also lord of that material cause.

Therefore, considering his ability, him being immanent or not immanent, him having a purpose or not having a purpose, and considering the nature of the cause, it is not correct [to claim that Īśvara is the creator].[36]

Asaṅga's half-brother Vasubandhu was also an influential Yogācāra philosopher. According to Indian and Tibetan legends about Vasubandhu's life, he

[36] Translated from the Sanskrit text in Bhattacharya 1957, 144–145.

started out as an adherent of the Sautrāntika school of Buddhism, a form of Theravāda, and then later converted to Mahāyāna due to his brother's influence.[37] In the *Abhidharmakośa*, one of Vasubandhu's work that seems to show the most Sautrāntika influence, Vasubandhu claims that the idea that Īśvara can be the cause of all things becomes untenable once one realizes that everything is subject to suffering, another version of the theodicy argument we saw earlier.[38]

The Ādibuddha: The Buddha as Creator?

If no god could have created the world, what about a buddha? The idea of an *Ādibuddha* ("primordial buddha") is found in some forms of Vajrayāna Buddhism, although it is foreign to most other forms of Buddhism. This primordial buddha, who is identified with figures such as the bodhisattva Samantabhadra, the buddha Vairocana, or the buddha Vajradhara, is a first and eternally enlightened buddha. This Ādibuddha encompasses both *saṃsāra* (the cycle of death and rebirth) and *nirvāṇa*, and although the phenomenal world arises from his consciousness, he is perceived quite differently from creator gods in other religious traditions. The world created by the Ādibuddha is not an absolutely real physical universe, but, rather, the physical universe is one of many temporary displays of the infinite awareness of the Ādibuddha.

The concept of an Ādibuddha is particularly prominent in the Atiyoga (Dzogchen) tradition of the Nyingma school of Tibetan Buddhism and of the Yungdrung Bön tradition of Tibet. Atiyoga ("the highest yoga") teaches that all phenomena are temporary manifestations that arise out of a primordial wisdom. This wisdom (*rigpa*) is the primordial ground of all things. In the Nyingma school, the Ādibuddha is identified with the bodhisattva Samantabhadra ("completely good"), and all phenomena are mere manifestations of Samantabhadra. He is depicted in art as a naked blue figure, representing the infinity of space and the absolute reality behind all changing forms. Samantabhadra is not a creator god in a physical sense, but rather the primordial ground of being, out of whose consciousness all phenomena arise. He is the primordial awareness.

The concept of an Ādibuddha is also important in Kālacakra ("Wheel of Time") tradition of Indo-Tibetan Buddhism. In Kālacakra Tantra, the world

37 A few modern scholars of Buddhism, most notably Stcherbatsky (1923, 2), Kimura (1929), and Frauwallner (1951), have suggested that there may have existed two different philosophers by the name of Vasubandhu. The idea of a second Vasubandhu is also attested in the Indian tradition; Yaśomitra's commentary to the *Abhidharmakośa* by Vasubandhu quotes another teacher referred to as *sthaviro Vasubandhur ācārya* ("The Old Master Vasubandhu").

38 5.8.IV. Text from Gokhale 1946, accessed at https://gretil.sub.uni-goettingen.de/gretil/1_sanskr/6_sastra/3_phil/buddh/vakobhku.htm.

arises out of the collective *karma* of all sentient beings. According to the Kālacakra Tantra, there are two ways of seeing the Ādibuddha: either as "the first to obtain buddhahood by means of the imperishable bliss characterized by perfect awakening in a single moment,"[39] or as a being who has been enlightened since beginningless time, a being that represents "the innate gnosis that pervades the minds of all sentient beings and stands as the basis of both samsara and nirvana."[40] The Ādibuddha is not to be understood as a deity, but rather as a symbol of an eternal awareness that is the ground of both the physical world and our own minds, an awareness that is radically different from a personal creator god.

3 Salvation without Gods

Although gods are more peripheral to Buddhism than to most other religious traditions, soteriology (a doctrine of salvation) is nevertheless central to Buddhist thought. But if a person is not saved by a deity, how is salvation possible? This section outlines the Theravāda Buddhist vision of enlightenment achieved purely through human agency, but also discusses the ways in which Mahāyāna Buddhism introduces the idea that extraordinary beings such as buddhas and bodhisattvas can function as saviors.

Salvation in Buddhism

Buddhism teaches that living beings are caught up in a karma-fueled cycle of death and rebirth, and that all existence within this cycle is characterized by dissatisfaction. Someone who has not reached enlightenment will be reborn again and again, in different states of existence, as a human being, animal, god, demon, ghost, or hell being. While rebirth as a god – which is the result of good karma – is a pleasant condition, it is entirely temporary and will come to an end once the good karma has been used up. Ultimately, the entire cycle of death and rebirth, called *saṃsāra*, is characterized by dissatisfaction (*dukkha*).

According to the teachings of the Buddha, all conditioned things are characterized by three marks or characteristics (*lakkhaṇa*): *aniccā* (impermanence), *dukkha* (dissatisfaction), and *anattā* (lack of self). Nothing in this world is eternal, nothing has a permanent essence, and that will eventually lead to dissatisfaction for those living beings who are attached to noneternal things.

The fact that all conditioned things are marked by *dukkha* (dissatisfaction, often translated as "suffering") does not mean that there is no joy or pleasure to be found in the world; Buddhists take as much delight in friendship, family, and

[39] Wallace 2001, 17. [40] Wallace 2001, 18.

pleasant experiences as anyone else. But despite these temporary pleasures, all conditioned things are ultimately unsatisfying because it is in their nature that they cannot last. Living beings may experience happiness, but if that happiness is based on assuming that impermanent things (such as human beings) will last forever, the happiness will eventually turn to dissatisfaction and suffering.

The ultimate goal for a Buddhist, therefore, is to become free from death and rebirth and obtain a state, *nibbāna* (*nirvāṇa*), characterized by an absence of all dissatisfaction. But *nibbāna* is, according to Theravāda Buddhism, a goal that living beings must reach for themselves, not through the intervention of a higher being or Buddha. The Theravāda Buddhist text *Dhammapada* states, for example, that "you yourself must make the effort. The Tathāgatas [buddhas] are only teachers."[41]

Not only are there no gods who save human beings in Buddhism; several Buddhist philosophers have argued that belief in an eternal god is nothing but a distraction for humans seeking enlightenment and salvation.

What Is Nibbāna?

Salvation in Buddhism involves attaining *nibbāna*. The Pāli term *nibbāna* (*nirvāṇa* in Sanskrit) literally means "blowing out" or "extinction," as in the blowing out of a flame or lamp. *Nibbāna* is also called *mokkha* (Sanskrit *mokṣa*, "freedom, release"). *Nibbāna* should not be understood as a place or even as a state, but rather as complete freedom from dissatisfaction and suffering. When *nibbāna* is achieved, a person is no longer reborn. The method for achieving this goal is outlined in the eightfold path (see Section 1). Significantly, salvation can be achieved through human effort, without the intervention of any superhuman being.

A Theravāda Buddhist distinguishes between four stages in the process of reaching enlightenment: A *sotāpanna* ("stream-enterer") is a person who has perceived the true teaching and entered the eightfold path. This person is free from the illusion of a permanent self, free from attachment to rituals, and free from doubt about the Buddha's teachings. The next stage is to become a *sakadāgamī* ("once-returner"), a person who only has one single worldly rebirth left before enlightenment. Such a person will have much less sensual desire and ill will than other people. An *anāgamī* ("non-returner") is completely free of sensory desire and ill will, and who will never be reborn again in the material realm after they die. The fourth and final stage is that of an *arahant* ("worthy one"; one who has obtained the highest goal of *nibbāna* in the current

[41] *Dhammapada* 276. Text from Radhakrishnan 1950, 146.

life). An *arahant* is not only free from desire and ill will, but also from any attachment to the four meditative absorptions, the four formless absorptions, conceit, restlessness, and ignorance.

This salvation is not necessarily accessible to all human beings in their current lifetime. According to Theravāda Buddhism, it is immensely difficult for a layperson to follow the eightfold path; ideally, a person seeking *nibbāna* in this lifetime needs to be a monk who can devote the necessary number of hours a day to meditation. What then of laypeople? Their best hope, in most forms of Theravāda Buddhism, is to perform good deeds, gain karmic merit, and hope to be reborn as a monk in their next life.

What happens to a person when they reach *nibbāna?* The Buddha himself is believed to have entered *nibbāna* upon his enlightenment under the *bodhi* tree, although he continued to live and teach for many years thereafter. Buddhist traditions differentiate between the Buddha's initial *nibbāna* and his later *parinibbāna* ("complete extinction"), which took place upon his death.

The term *nirvāṇa* is also used in Hinduism to characterize liberation from the cycle of death and rebirth, but the description of this state differs greatly in Hindu and Buddhist scripture. While Hindu texts describe salvation as a state of bliss consisting of union between the individual self (*ātman*) and the cosmic divine force of *brahman*, Buddhism teaches that there is no self that can experience such a union.

But if there is no self in Buddhism, who or what is it that experiences *nibbāna?* The answer is: no one. The very concept of a self is an illusion in Buddhism, and enlightenment is only possible once this illusion is dissolved. Upon reaching a state of *nibbāna*, there is no longer even the illusion of a self. While *nibbāna* is described as the highest bliss in Buddhist texts, it is an experience without the illusion of an experiencer.

Nibbāna is often defined in Buddhist texts as the end of dissatisfaction (*dukkha*). Since dissatisfaction is caused by desire, *nibbāna* also implies an end of all desires. But is *nibbāna* then merely an absence of something, rather than something in itself? The Pāli canon is quite explicit that this is not the case; *nibbāna* is an *atthi-dhamma*, an element of existence, rather than a mere absence.[42]

The Buddha defines *nibbāna* as follows:

> Thus have I heard. One time, the Blessed One was staying at Sāvatthi in the Jeta forest at the Anāthapiṇḍika monastery. At that time, the Blessed One taught, roused, inspired, and delighted the monks with a discourse on *dhamma* focused on nibbāna. The monks, attentive and concentrated were

[42] See discussion in Collins 2010, 47.

focused on listening to the *dhamma*. The Blessed One, understanding its impact, then said at that time this inspired speech:

"There is, monks, a sphere where there is no earth, no water, no heat and no wind, where the sphere of infinite space does not exist, or the sphere of infinite consciousness, or that which is neither perception nor non-perception. It is not this world, nor is it another world, nor is it both. It is neither the sun nor the moon. Here, monks, I tell you that there is no coming or going, no staying, no cessation or arising. It is neither fixed nor moving, and it has no support. This, indeed, is the end of dissatisfaction."[43]

Although *nibbāna* is described here mainly in terms of what it is not, the text makes perfectly clear that *nibbāna* itself is something that exists ("There is, monks, a sphere . . . "). The sphere of *nibbāna* is ultimately real, although it is impossible to capture in the language that is used to describe things that are of this world.

What does it mean to call *nibbāna* a "sphere" (*āyatana*)? This term, which can also be translated as "base" or "field" designates a sphere of sensory cognition in Buddhism. Buddhist texts identify twelve of these spheres, six internal and six internal. The six internal *āyatanas* are the six sense organs: the eye, the ear, the nose, the tongue, the body, and the mind.[44] The six external *āyatanas* are the corresponding sense-objects: visible objects, founds, smells, tastes, tangible objects, and thoughts. What does it mean, then, when *nibbāna* itself is also designated as an *āyatana?* The craving or desire that is the very origin of dissatisfaction originates from the contact between the six internal *āyatanas* with the six external ones. Characterizing *nirvāṇa* itself as an *āyatana*, although a very different one from the regular twelve, suggests the possibility of a form of experience that does not lead to desire or dissatisfaction. When the *āyatanas* are seen as impermanent, however, there is no resulting desire:

A monk came up to the Blessed One, greeted him respectfully, sat down to one side, and said to him: "Sir, how should a person know or see in order for the fetters to be abandoned?" "Monk, when one knows and sees the eye as impermanent, the fetters are abandoned. When one knows and sees forms as impermanent, the fetters are abandoned. [. . .] When one knows and sees as impermanent that feeling that arises from contact with the mind, whether it's pleasant or unpleasant or neither, the fetters are abandoned. When one knows and sees in this way, monk, the fetters are abandoned."[45]

---

[43] *Udāna* 8.1 of the *Khuddaka Nikāya*, translation based on the text of the Pali Text Society online at www.accesstoinsight.org/tipitaka/sltp/Ud_utf8.html#pts.080.

[44] The mind (*manas*) is regarded as one of the sense organs in both Buddhist and Hindu philosophy. This "sixth sense" is nothing supernatural; rather, our mind is regarded as a sense organ in the same way that eyes and ears are. Just like the eye perceives visible objects and the ear perceives audible objects, so the mind perceives thinkable objects (thoughts).

[45] *Saṃyutta Nikāya* 35.53–54. Text from Feer 1894, 30–31.

A person who has reached *nibbāna* is called an *arahant*, or, more rarely, a *buddha*, an enlightened one. In Theravāda Buddhism, then, the Buddha is not a savior, but, rather, salvation is becoming a buddha oneself. In Buddhism, there are numerous buddhas, not just one, all characterized by the attainment of a state of absolute freedom from dissatisfaction.

When a person has obtained *nibbāna*, what happens to that person after death? When asked this question, the Buddha answered:

> As a flame is extinguished by the wind,
> vanishes and can no longer be perceived,
> so a sage free from name and form
> vanishes and can no longer be perceived.
> One cannot perceive one who has been extinguished.
> There is no way to describe someone without attributes.
> All ways to speak about them have vanished.[46]

We should note that the Buddha does not say that the enlightened person no longer exists in *nibbāna*, but rather, that they are free of all attributes that can be described by human language. Categories like existence and nonexistence are simply no longer applicable.

Many Buddhist texts refer to *nibbāna* as indescribable. And yet, there is no shortage of textual passages that analyze this ineffable state in detail. Although *nibbāna* cannot be adequately described, it is frequently called "bliss" and "joy" and "the highest joy" in Buddhist texts. It is described in Buddhist texts as the "highest happiness,"[47] but it is radically different from other forms of happiness that revolve around sense pleasures and a false sense of self.

This usage may have influenced our everyday usage of *nibbāna* or *nirvāṇa* as "bliss"; one tea company used to advertise its products, for example, as "nirvana in a cup." But *nirvāṇa* cannot be understood as similar to the kind of pleasure a person experiences during a lifetime; rather, it is a radically other state and radically other kind of joy. In Theravada, this state is wished for oneself and for others whom one likewise wishes will one day escape suffering.

Nirvāṇa and Bodhisattvas in Mahāyāna Buddhism

In Mahāyāna Buddhism, the goal is not just the attainment of *nirvāṇa* for oneself, but rather the attainment of *nirvāṇa* for all sentient beings. As mentioned previously, a bodhisattva is someone who has reached enlightenment but stops at the very brink of *nirvāṇa* and chooses to be reborn again in the suffering

---

[46] *Khuddaka Nikāya* 5: *Sutta-Nipāta* 5.6. Text from the Pali Text Society online at www.accesstoinsight.org/ati/tipitaka/sltp/Sn_utf8.html#v.1069.

[47] *Dhammapada* 204, text from Radhakrishnan 1950, 127.

world in order to help bring other sentient beings to enlightenment as well. Consequently, a bodhisattva functions as a savior of sorts in Mahāyāna Buddhism. While a bodhisattva is not a god, he, she, or it is a being who has reached enlightenment and whose goal is to ease the suffering of all others. While other living beings are reborn as a result of their *karma,* bodhisattvas are reborn out of their own free will, in whatever form (human or animal) that they deem most conducive to freeing others from the cycle of death and rebirth.

A bodhisattva's path is fundamentally different from the eightfold path taught by the Buddha. First of all, a bodhisattva must develop what is called *bodhicitta* ("thought of enlightenment"), which is a deep compassion toward all other living beings and a yearning to strive for their enlightenment. A bodhisattva will further develop the qualities necessary to become a buddha, which are called the "perfections" (*pāramitā*): giving (*dāna*), morality (*śīla*), patience (*kṣānti*), energy (*vīrya*), contemplation (*dhyāna*), and wisdom (*prajñā*).

A bodhisattva has as his or her goal the enlightenment and salvation of all living beings:

> This is the intention of a bodhisattva. A glow worm or some other luminous insect does not think of its light illuminating and shining over the whole continent of the Rose Apple Tree [India]. Similarly, the Śrāvakas [Buddhist disciples] and Pratyekabuddhas [buddhas who reach enlightenment through their own efforts] do not think of leading all living beings to *nirvāṇa* after reaching enlightenment. But when the sun has risen, it illuminates all of the continent of the Rose Apple Tree. In the same way, a bodhisattva who has completed the practices that reach to buddhahood, leads countless sentient beings to *nirvāṇa.*[48]

Nāgārjuna's Paradox: Samsāra is Nirvāṇa

So far, we have discussed the concept of *nirvāṇa* as the liberation from *saṃsāra*. But what if *nirvāṇa* and *saṃsāra* are ultimately not different from one another? The 2nd-century Mahāyāna Buddhist philosopher Nāgārjuna devoted a whole chapter (chapter 25) of his most well-known work *Mūlamadhyamakakārikā* ("The Root Verses of the Middle Way") to a discussion of *nirvāṇa*. He writes:

> *Nirvāṇa* is not a thing, because then it would be characterized by old age and death, and no thing is free from old age and death.[49]
>
> The state of moving about restlessly (in *saṃsāra*) is dependent and conditioned, but that which is independent and unconditioned, is *nirvāṇa*.[50]

[48] *Pañcaviṁśatisāhasrikā* 41. Text from Dutt 1934, 168–169.
[49] *Mūlamadhyamakakārikā* 25.4. Text from La Vallée Poussin 1913, 522.
[50] *Mūlamadhyamakakārikā* 25.9. Text from La Vallée Poussin 1913, 529.

These are statements that most Buddhist could easily agree with; *nirvāṇa* is different from all conditioned things, including *saṃsāra*. And yet, in a different section of this chapter, Nāgārjuna writes:

> *Saṃsāra* is not different from *nirvāṇa,* and *nirvāṇa* is not different from *saṃsāra*. The limit of *nirvāṇa* is also the limit of *saṃsāra,* and there is no difference whatsoever between the two.[51]

At first sight, this is a stunning statement. How can the Buddhist philosopher possibly equate *nirvāṇa* and *saṃsāra*, when *nirvāṇa* is defined as the extinction of the suffering that characterizes *saṃsāra?* It is possible to read Nāgārjuna's enigmatic equation of *saṃsāra* and *nirvāṇa* as implying that the two concepts represent the same reality, seen from two completely different perspectives, one unenlightened and one enlightened. For someone who is trapped in a conventional way of thinking, the reality in which we live is *saṃsāra*, but for someone who sees things as they truly are, the same reality is *nirvāṇa*. Nāgārjuna writes about these two ways of looking at reality:

The teaching of the *dharma* by the buddhas is based on two truths:

> Conventional truth and the truth from the perspective of the highest reality.[52]

For Nāgārjuna, conventional truth is our everyday conventional reality, where people and objects are assumed to be real and have some sort of continuous existence, while the higher truth is associated with the insight that both people and objects lack permanence and substance, with every element of their existence being characterized by interdependence or emptiness. *Nirvāṇa* is not, therefore, a different form of existence from our ordinary everyday lives, but rather our ordinary reality transformed by the insight that this reality is ultimately a construct. Salvation, therefore, implies a shift in perspective, rather than an entrance into a different reality.

Salvation and Buddha-Fields

But Mahāyāna Buddhism also operates with the idea of other worlds. According to Mahāyāna Buddhism, there exist numerous parallel realms, each with its own buddha. A particular buddha's realm or sphere of influence is called a buddha field (*buddhakṣetra*). A buddha field is a realm or dimension of space-time where there is a buddha who teaches the *dharma* to living beings out of compassion. There are three kinds of buddha fields, pure, impure, and mixed. The historical Buddha, Śakyamuni, presides over a buddha-field called Sahā

[51] *Mūlamadhyamakakārikā* 25.19. Text from La Vallée Poussin 1913, 535.
[52] *Mūlamadhyamakakārikā* 24.8. Text from La Vallée Poussin 1913, 492.

("That which must be endured"). But how can the buddha field presided over by a perfect buddha itself be imperfect? Some Buddhist texts argue that our buddha field *is* pure; it just appears to be impure to those who have not yet purified their own mind. Others argue that the Buddha deliberately chose to be reborn in an impure buddha field out of compassion.[53]

While the idea is found in many Mahāyāna texts from India, the notion of buddha fields was developed further in the Pure Land traditions of Mahāyāna Buddhism, which are popular in East Asia. A Pure Land is a buddha field that has been purified and cleansed of all defilements by the buddha who dwells in it. Sentient beings can be reborn in pure buddha fields due to accumulation of good karma. A person reborn in a Pure Land is believed to be able to reach *nirvāṇa* more easily due to the positive influence of the buddha who has created the buddha field Particularly popular is the Pure Land called *Sukhāvatī* ("The blissful one") which is ruled over by the buddha Amitābha.

According to the *Large Sūtra of Immeasurable Life*, Amitābha was once upon a time a monk, or perhaps a king, called Dharmākara. He resolved to become a buddha and made a series of forty-eight vows that involve the creation of a pure land, *Sukhāvatī* ("the Blissful One"). The eighteenth vow (according to East Asian versions of the text) is that anyone who calls his name with sincerity will be reborn in his pure land. He also vowed to appear in front of anyone who calls upon him at the moment of death. Amitābha ("infinite splendor") is venerated throughout China, Korea, Vietnam, Japan, and Tibet. It is generally believed that to be reborn in Amitābha's paradise of *Sukhāvatī*, all a person must do is call upon Amitābha by name, an idea first mentioned in the Sanskrit *Pratyutpanna Samādhi Sūtra* (ca. 1st century BCE to 2nd century CE):

> Bodhisattvas hear about the buddha Amitābha and call him to mind again and again in this land. Because of this calling to mind, they see the buddha Amitābha. Having seen him they ask him what dharmas it takes to be born in the realm of the buddha Amitābha. Then the buddha Amitābha says to these bodhisattvas: "If you wish to come and be born in my realm, you must always call me to mind again and again, you must always keep this thought in mind without letting up, and thus you will succeed in coming to be born in my realm."[54]

Amitābha is also described in three popular Indian Mahayana texts, the 1st- to 2nd-century CE *Longer Sukhāvatīvyūha Sūtra* and *Shorter Sukhāvatīvyūha Sūtra,* and the 5th-century-CE *Amitāyurdhyāna Sūtra* ("The Amitāyur Meditation Sūtra"). According to the *Longer Sukhāvatīvyūha Sūtra* (also known as the *Sūtra on Immeasurable Life*), a young man named Dharmākara meets the buddha Lokeśvara and is so overwhelmed by this encounter that he

[53] Williams 2008, 217. [54] Harrison and McRae 1998, 22–23.

makes forty-eight solemn vows, including the vow to create a Pure Land that can be accessed by anyone who calls his name. Through numerous rebirths, Dharmākara is able to fulfil all the vows, and he becomes the buddha Amitābha.

Are the buddhas venerated in the Pure Land tradition savior figures? Not precisely. A person reborn in the Pure Land must still strive for *nirvāṇa,* but the buddha of that realm has created optimal conditions for reaching enlightenment. A person's attainment of *nirvāṇa* in dependent on the aid of a buddha in Pure Land Buddhism, although there still has to be some minimal effort on the part of the person seeking enlightenment. With the help of compassionate buddhas, however, the path toward *nirvāṇa* is made as easy as it can possibly be.

Merit transfer is one of the many forms of help buddhas offer in Pure Land Buddhism. While *karma* is something individual that cannot be transferred from buddhas to others in most forms of Theravāda Buddhism,[55] the buddhas can and do share their karmic merit with others in Pure Land Buddhism. The karmic merit that a buddha has obtained can be transferred to other suffering beings who need merit to obtain a favorable rebirth in a pure land. Salvation, in Pure Land Buddhism, cannot take place in this flawed world; but it is both possible and easy to obtain in a Pure Land. Rebirth in a Pure Land is possible through faith in a bodhisattva such as Amitābha. But even though Amitābha is worshipped in the Pure Land schools of China and Japan, he is not perceived as a creator or ruler of the world.

Salvation in the *Lotus Sūtra*

The *Lotus Sūtra* (*Saddharmapuṇḍarīkasūtra* in Sanskrit, *Myōhō Renge Kyō* in Japanese) is a Mahāyāna text that has been particularly influential in East Asia, and it has been translated into Chinese, Tibetan, Mongolian, Manchu, Tangut, Korean, Vietnamese, and Japanese. The precise date and original language of the *Lotus Sūtra* is the subject of some debate. The text was first translated into Chinese in the 3rd century of the Common Era, likely from Sanskrit, although the original version may have been in a different language.

The *Lotus Sūtra* teaches that all Buddhist paths – including those of a Theravāda monk and of a Mahāyāna bodhisattva – lead to buddhahood. According to the *Lotus Sūtra*, even simple forms of devotion such as chanting the name of the buddha, can lead to buddhahood and *nirvāṇa.*

Salvation is accessible to all according to the *Lotus Sūtra*, and the text contains long passages where the Buddha describes the future buddhahood

[55] There are exceptions to this, however. Funerary rituals are often intended to create merit for the dead, and the text *Petavatthu* in the Pāli Canon describes merit-making on behalf of the dead through gift-giving and feeding monks in great detail.

that awaits his family members, disciples and friends, and even his evil cousin Devadatta, who is often presented as the antagonist in other Buddhist texts, opposing the Buddha's teachings at every turn. But in the *Lotus Sūtra,* buddhahood awaits even Devadatta. Another surprising enlightenment in the *Lotus Sūtra* is that of the eight-year-old daughter of the king of the Nāgas, a race of mythical serpents. The message of the text is clearly that salvation is accessible to everyone, regardless of their past actions, age, gender, or even species.

The *Lotus Sūtra* teaches that the Buddha is not gone from the world after his death, but that his physical death was a mere illusion, and that the Buddha is still present in the world, accessible to devotees, and able to teach the *dharma* that will bring them to salvation. The Buddha of the *Lotus Sūtra* is therefore quite removed from the human Siddhāttha Gotama of the Pāli canon; he is an eternal being who strives for the salvation of all living beings.

Salvation and Buddha Nature

Although the *Lotus Sūtra* does not use the term, many later commentators and scholars have seen in this text the beginnings of a doctrine of buddha nature, an idea more fully developed in the text called the *Tathāgatagarbha Sūtra* ("The Womb of Buddhahood *Sūtra*"). Although this text was likely first composed in Sanskrit, it has only survived in Tibetan and Chinese translations.

Tathāgatagarbha ("buddha embryo," or "buddha nature") is the innate potential in all living beings for buddhahood. According to this doctrine, all living beings contain an eternal buddha-essence within, an essence that can shine forth when the mind is cleansed of its impurities and defilements. The idea of a *Tathāgatagarbha* is a further development of the idea of the luminous mind (*prabhāsvaracitta*) encountered in the Pāli canon, a pure form of consciousness that has temporarily been defiled by impurities. The *Buddhāvataṃsaka Sūtra* ("The Garland of Buddhas Sūtra"), a Mahāyāna text, describes how the wisdom of the Buddha is present in all beings. Salvation is therefore conceived of not as a radical change from an unenlightened state to an enlightened one, but rather as an uncovering of a primordial wisdom that is already present, but occluded, in living beings.

Salvation in Nichiren Buddhism

Nichiren Buddhism (also called Hokkeshū or "Lotus Sect" Buddhism) is a branch of Mahāyāna Buddhism based on the teachings of the 13th-century Japanese Buddhist priest Nichiren. Nichiren (1222–1282) claimed that only the *Lotus Sūtra* was a suitable Buddhist text for the Third Age of Buddhism. Many Mahāyāna schools view the history of Buddhism as divided into three ages: the Former Day of the Dharma, the first millennium after the Buddha when his disciples were able to transmit his teachings accurately; the Middle Day of the Dharma, the second millennium after the Buddha when the knowledge of the right doctrine began to fade; and the Latter Day of the Dharma or the Third Age, when the Buddha's teachings are in decline. During the decline of the Third Age, people are no longer able to grasp the original teachings of Buddhism, and a simpler and more direct method is called for.

Nichiren Buddhism claims that all living beings possess buddha nature, and that they can therefore attain buddhahood in this life. Nichiren Buddhist practice involves venerating objects (usually scrolls or statues) called *gohonzon* through the chant *Namu Myōhō Renge Kyō* ("Glory to the *dharma* of the *Lotus Sūtra*"). Although the *Lotus Sūtra* is venerated in Nichiren Buddhism, the focus is not on studying the entire text or its teachings, but rather on chanting the very name of the text. Chanting the *Namu Myōhō Renge Kyō* mantra repeatedly is in itself seen as a path to salvation in Nichiren Buddhism.

Salvation in Zen Buddhism

A form of Mahāyāna, Zen Buddhism originated in India, but soon spread to East Asia, and is today most popular in Japan. The name "Zen" is a Japanese version of *chán,* the Chinese pronunciation of the Sanskrit term *dhyāna* ("meditation"). The mythical founder of Zen Buddhism is the monk Bodhidharma. Incorporating the idea of a buddha nature present in all living beings, Zen Buddhism postulates that there are two ways to uncover this inherent buddha nature and reach salvation, slow enlightenment (cp. the arduous eightfold path) and sudden enlightenment. While some claimed that the buddha nature can be realized gradually, others argued for the notion of "sudden enlightenment."

In Japanese Zen Buddhism, *satori*, or awakening, is an understanding of one's own nature. This understanding is brought about by a shift in perspective that involves un-learning accepted "truths" about the conditioned reality. This shift in perspective can be brought about in a single moment, if one's mind is shocked into an awareness of the absurdity of what we believe to be our everyday reality. Zen riddles, or *koans*, are thought to be helpful in bringing about this sudden shift in thinking pattern. Perhaps the most well-known example of a *koan* is the question "What is the sound of one hand clapping?" Like all *koans*, this riddle is meant to be unanswerable; "clapping" is normally defined as bringing two hands together, so pondering the sound of one hand clapping is meant to help the student unravel the all-too-comfortable notion that the conditioned reality that we experience in our daily lives and describe through language actually makes sense. In this case, the path to salvation is in the deconstruction of our conventional ways of thinking.

4 The Roles of Gods, Buddhas, and Bodhisattvas

The section compares the roles of gods with those of enlightened buddhas and bodhisattvas in Buddhism. While gods may have superhuman powers, they cannot bring anyone to enlightenment, unless they themselves become buddhas and bodhisattvas. But if a buddha or a bodhisattva can help bring other beings to salvation, do they themselves function as gods in Buddhism?

Gods in Buddhist Texts

There are two different words for gods used in Pāli and Sanskrit Buddhist texts: *deva* and *brahmā*. Both types of deities are largely borrowed from Hinduism, but in Buddhism they are not eternal beings. Rather, both *devas* and *brahmās* are divine but impermanent beings, caught up in the cycle of death and reincarnation. A *brahmā* is a different, more subtle type of *deva*, but still noneternal and without the power to save anyone.

Although there are gods in Buddhism, the gods themselves must learn that they are impermanent. As it says in the *Aṅguttara-Nikāya*:

> The Blessed One arises in the world, holy, fully enlightened, endowed with knowledge and good conduct, sublime, the knower of worlds, the incomparable leader of men in need of guidance, the teacher of gods and men, enlightened and blessed. He teaches the *dhamma*: "This is the ego, this is the origin of the ego, this is the cessation of the ego, this is the way that leads to the cessation of the ego."
>
> And the gods, long-lived, beautiful, who dwell happily and for a long time in heavenly palaces, hear him teach the *dhamma*, and they become fearful, agitated, and trembling: "We believed that we were permanent, even though we are actually impermanent. We believed that we were everlasting, even though we are actually fleeting. We believed that we were eternal, even though we are actually non-eternal. But we are impermanent, fleeting, non-eternal, steeped in ego."[56]

A humorous passage in the *Dīgha Nikāya* features a monk who is trying to learn about the nature of reality from a deity, "the great Brahmā":

> Shortly thereafter, Kevaddha, the great Brahmā appeared. The monk came up to him and asked: "My friend, where do the four great elements of earth, water, fire, and air, cease to exist, leaving no trace behind?" The great Brahmā answered: "Monk, I am Brahmā, the great Brahmā, the supreme, powerful, all-seeing, the ruler and lord of all, the controller, the creator, the sovereign of all, putting everything in its place, the ancient one, the father of all that is and all that will be." The monk asked Brahmā again: "Friend, I did not ask you

[56] *Sīha Sutta, Catukka-nipāta, Cakkavagga*, 33, *Aṅguttara Nikāya*. Text from Morris 1888 (1955), 33–34.

> whether you are Brahmā, the great Brahmā [...], but where the four great elements of earth, water, fire, and air, cease to exist, leaving no trace behind?" But again, Brahmā answered, "I am Brahmā, the great Brahmā ... " [...]. [...] Then the great Brahmā took the monk by the arm and led him aside and said: "Monk, these gods in the Brahmā world believe that there is nothing I cannot see, nothing I don't know, and nothing that is not manifest to me. Therefore, I didn't answer you in front of them. I don't know, monk, where the four great elements of earth, water, fire, and air, cease to exist, leaving no trace behind. [...] Go to the Blessed One [the Buddha], ask him your question, and accept his answer."[57]

Here, Brahmā himself has to admit that he has no idea what the answer to the monk's question might be and recommends that he asks the Buddha instead. The Hindu creator god Brahmā is also featured in narratives about the enlightenment of Siddhattha; he is the one who begs the Buddha to teach his insights to others after his enlightenment.[58]

According to Buddhism, even the gods will eventually die. Although they live longer lifespans than humans, they are not eternal. Unlike humans, however, gods do not get sick before they die; their impending death is signaled by other changes: their clothes will get dirty, their flower garlands will wither, they will begin to sweat, their bodies will no longer be shiny, and they will begin to sit restlessly. Gods will die when they have run out of their allotted life spans, or even because they forget to eat.[59] Although gods are superhuman, they are far less significant in Buddhism than buddhas or bodhisattvas.

Who Is the Buddha in Buddhism?

The Buddha is presented in Buddhist texts as a human being, a mortal man, but at the same time, he is more than an ordinary human. Buddhist texts claim that one cannot say that the Buddha exists after death, but also not that he does not exist, and not that he both exists and doesn't exist, or that he neither exists nor does not exist. He is, simply put, someone who has transcended ordinary forms of existence.

A Brahman asked the Buddha whether he was a god or a spirit or a ghost, and the Buddha said no. But asked whether he was human, the Buddha, surprisingly, also said no:

> One time, the Lord [the Buddha] was traveling along the high road between Ukkattha and Setabbya, and so was the Brahman Dona. Dona approached the Lord and said: "Sir, are you a *deva*?" "No, Brahman, I am not a *deva*." "Are

[57] *Kevaddha Sutta, Dīgha Nikāya* 11.81–83, text from Rhys Davids and Carpenter 1975, 220–222.

[58] *Ariyapariyesana Sutta* of the *Majjhima-nikaya*, text from Trenckner 1979, 168–169.

[59] Malalasekara 1937, 1119.

> you a *gandharva*?" "No, Brahman." "Are you a *yakkha*?" "No, Brahman, I am not a *yakkha*." "Then are you a human being, sir?" "No, Brahman, I am not a human being." "You say no to all my questions. So who are you, sir?" "Brahman, those outflows through which, if they had not been extinguished, I might have been a *deva*, a *gandharva*, a *yakkha*, or a human being, those outflows are extinguished in me, cut off at the root like the stump of a palm tree that will not come into existence again in the future. Like a blue lotus, a red lotus, or a white lotus, born in water and grown in water, rises above the water and stands unsullied by the water, so do I, Brahman, born in the world and grown in the world, rise above the world and stand unsullied by the world. Know that I am a buddha."[60]

A buddha is, after his enlightenment, different from both gods and humans, but he is not unique. Anyone who attains to the same insights can similarly become a buddha, a being that transcends both humanity and divinity.

According to Buddhist tradition, Siddhattha Gotama is not the first, nor the last, buddha to live. But the Buddha does have supernatural powers, and he is venerated at Buddhist shrines. Hindus see him as an incarnation (*avatāra*) of the god Viṣṇu, but Buddhists do not. The Buddha is revered in Buddhism, not because of a divine origin or nature, but because of extraordinary attainments and his teachings, which have the potential to lead others out of dissatisfaction and suffering. But although his followers venerate him, the Buddha is not believed to hear them; he is no longer a part of the world of the living.

The Pāli canon tells of the life of the Buddha, but his biography also encompasses many previous lives, which are recorded in the stories called *Jātakas*. The Jātakas tell of the Buddha's past lives as various animals and human beings. These narratives underscore that even Siddhattha Gotama had to go through many lives in order to reach enlightenment. The Buddha is unique among the characters in the Pāli Canon, but not in the world; there have been many buddhas before him, and there will be many other buddhas after.

The Buddha is, however, an extraordinary human being. Several Buddhist texts list the thirty-two marks (*lakkhaṇa*) of beauty characterizing a Buddha's body.[61] These marks include having webbed hands and feet, the mark of a wheel under the soles of the feet, golden skin, white teeth, blue eyes, and eyelashes resembling those of a cow. While some of these characteristics can be found in ordinary human beings, others, like the mark of a wheel under the soles of the feet, signal the Buddha's extraordinary nature. A buddha also possesses omniscience (*sarvajñatva*), a quality usually only ascribed to gods.[62] But the

[60] *Aṅguttara Nikāya* 4.36, *Doṇaloka Sutta*, text from Morris 1888 (1955), 37–39.

[61] See for example the *Lakkhaṇa Sutta*, *Dīgha Nikāya 30.* Text from Carpenter 1911 (1960), 142–179.

[62] See Jaini 1974.

Buddha's omniscience is not a trait he is born with, but rather one that he has acquired. In the *Milinda-pañho* ("The Questions of King Milinda"), King Milinda asks the venerable Nāgasena whether the Buddha was omniscient. The monk answers:

> Yes, your majesty, the Buddha was omniscient. But this insight was not always present in him; the omniscience of the Blessed One arose from reflection. By reflection, he knew what he wanted to know.[63]

But even though he is omniscient, the Buddha is not perceived as a creator, and he cannot change the fundamental laws of the cosmos.

Was the Buddha a human being? For the Theravāda and Sarvāstivāda schools of Buddhism, the answer is a firm yes. But as noted in the last section, the 2nd-century-CE Mahāyāna text *The Lotus Sūtra* depicts the Buddha as more of a supernatural being, and his human life is here presented as a mere illusion that allows him to teach the path to salvation.

The Three Bodies of the Buddha

The Mahāyāna doctrine of the three bodies (*trikāya*) of the Buddha explains the various roles of the Buddha in Mahāyāna, as a mortal man and a representation of the ultimate reality. A buddha possesses three different "bodies": (1) *Nirmāṇa-kāya* ("transformation body"), (2) *Saṃbhoga-kāya* ("enjoyment body"), and (3) *Dharma- kaya* ("dharma body"). The "transformation body" is a buddha's physical incarnation, or the human body the buddha inhabits. This body is not ultimately real, but a mere manifestation adopted due to compassion with the suffering world. The "enjoyment body" is a divine or supernatural incarnation of the buddha, obtained due to his karma from previous lives, while the "dharma body" is the ultimate reality represented by the buddha, beyond personhood. This dharma body is identified with *bodhi*, *nirvāṇa*, *śūnyatā*, and *tathātā*. It is also identified with buddha nature (*tathāgatagarbha*) present in all beings, which can develop into buddhahood. This idea is first articulated in the *Prajñāpāramitā*, and later systematized in the Yogācāra school of Mahāyāna Buddhist philosophy.

Bodhisattvas

The word *bodhisattva* (literally: "enlightenment being" means something different in Theravāda and Mahāyāna Buddhism. In Theravāda Buddhism, a bodhisattva is simply a future buddha, someone who has not yet appeared to teach the doctrine of the eightfold path, but who will do so in the future.

[63] Text from Trenckner 1880, 102.

According to Buddhism, there have been other buddhas before Siddhattha Gotama, and there will be others after him. According to Pāli Theravāda texts, the next buddha to appear in this world will be called Metteya (Sanskrit Maitreya, "the kind one"). For now, Metteya dwells in a heaven called Tusita (Sanskrit Tuṣita). Tusita is full of joy and satisfaction, and devoid of suffering. When Metteya is born on earth, he will obtain buddhahood under a tree in a flower garden, and he will save all sentient beings with three lectures on *dhamma*. Maitreya/Metteya is the only bodhisattva that is revered by both Theravāda and Mahāyāna Buddhists. While some Theravāda Buddhists pray that they will be reborn on earth when Maitreya lives, Mahāyāna Buddhist believe that one can be reborn in Tusita any time due to meritorious actions, and that it is also possible to visit Tusita during meditation while still living on earth.

In Mahāyāna Buddhism, the term bodhisattva takes on a new meaning. Here, a bodhisattva is someone who has already reached enlightenment for themselves, or is on the verge of doing so, but who chooses to be reborn into the suffering world to teach the path to enlightenment. Usually, as person's birth is caused by past deeds (*karma*) or defilements (*kleśa*). The next rebirth of a bodhisattva, however, is caused by his or her own will and completely free of any karmic baggage and mental defilements. A bodhisattva is reborn fully mindful and conscious.

Maitreya is also a bodhisattva in Mahāyāna Buddhism but is interpreted differently from the buddha-in-waiting of Theravāda; he is an enlightened figure who can reveal himself to his devotees here and now. According to Mahāyāna legends, Maitreya revealed himself to the Yogācāra philosopher Asaṅga. Asaṅga had meditated in the hopes of obtaining a vision of Maitreya, but to no avail. Disheartened, he walked along the road when he came across a suffering dog. He immediately stopped to help the dog, and it turned out that his compassion for another sentient being brought about the result that all his earnest meditation could not: the dog revealed himself to be Maitreya, and he gave him five texts, texts that are today ascribed to Asaṅga, but ultimately believed to be authored by Maitreya himself. When the Yogācāra school of Mahāyāna Buddhist philosophy spread to China, it also carried with it the cult of Maitreya.

The worship of Maitreya was particularly popular in Kashmir and spread to Central Asia and China. The Chinese traveler Fa-hsien, who visited India in the 5th century CE, records a legend he heard in India of a sculptor who was carried off to the Tuṣita heaven, where he saw Maitreya himself. Upon his return to earth, he created an enormous statue of Maitreya in northern Kashmir, a statue that was said to emit light on fast days. Such mystical visions of Maitreya are a part of Kashmir Buddhism, and in Gandhāran art, Maitreya is one of the most popular Buddhist figures depicted, next to Śakyamuni himself. The "laughing buddha" statues popular in China represent a Chinese form of Maitreya.

One of the most popular bodhisattvas in Mahāyāna is Avalokiteśvara ("the one who looks down (with compassion)"). Avalokiteśvara can appear as a man, woman, monk, layperson, buddha, or a nonhuman. According to Tibetan Buddhist texts, Avalokiteśvara even became a bird so that the birds could hear the Buddhist doctrine as well. The Dalai Lamas of Tibet are regarded as incarnations of Avalokiteśvara. Avalokiteśvara is called Kuan-yin in China and Kannon in Japan and reinterpreted as a female figure in East Asia.

Tārā is a popular female bodhisattva (sometimes buddha or goddess) in Tibet. She is closely associated with Avalokiteśvara. According to Tibetan legend, Avalokiteśvara was in despair because he didn't know how to save every living being. From the teardrop of his compassion, Tārā was born. She is often regarded as a fully enlightened buddha, or as the mother of all buddhas. Even though she is seen as a maternal figure, she is also depicted as eternally young, around sixteen years of age.

Mañjuśrī ("gentle glory") is the bodhisattva of wisdom (*prajñā*). He is very popular in early Mahāyāna texts, such as the *Prajñāparamitā Sūtras*. The later *Lotus Sūtra* claims that Mañjuśrī has a Pure Land called Vimala ("Faultless"), located in the east. In art, he is depicted holding a flaming sword, which represents his wisdom cutting through ignorance.

The bodhisattva Samantabhadra ("Completely Worthy") is called Pǔxián in Chinese and Fugen in Japanese. The *Samantabhadra Meditation Sūtra,* a text that is sometimes considered an epilogue to the *Lotus Sūtra,* describes Samantrabhadra's limitless form, which he can shrink down to human form when visiting this world. He is often depicted riding on a white elephant, which is considered identical to the elephant that appeared to Siddhattha Gotama's mother in a dream before she gave birth to the future Buddha.

A bodhisattva who has cultivated six perfections (see Section 3) will have supernatural powers that far transcend the capabilities of regular humans. This does not make a bodhisattva a deity, but a bodhisattva can function as a savior in Mahāyāna Buddhism. A bodhisattva's role in Buddhism can be compared in some respects to that of Christ in Christianity, but there are also significant differences. While Christians may strive to become more Christ-like, there can only be one Christ in Christianity. In Buddhism, however, the path of the bodhisattva is open to any being – human or other – who feels compassion for all living beings.

5 Gods and Goddesses in Buddhism

This section surveys the many minor deities that are mentioned in Buddhist texts and examines their roles in the Buddhist canon. While these deities are never involved in a person's enlightenment, they often function as high-ranking admirers or adversaries of the Buddha, examples of nonenlightened beings, or as exemplary wisdom seekers turning to the Buddha for answers.

While deities are peripheral to the Pāli canon of Theravāda Buddhism, many gods and goddesses have later become part of popular Buddhist belief and practice. This section discusses the many gods and goddesses that are worshipped in the popular Buddhism of Sri Lanka, Tibet, and Japan, and what these forms of worship mean for our understanding of what "Buddhism" is. As we will see, older Hindu deities were often incorporated into Buddhism, and local folk deities also occupy an important position in popular Buddhist worship.

Although gods may be powerful, Buddhist texts make quite clear that being a god is not the best possible form of existence. The *Dhammapada* claims that even the gods envy a human being whose senses are controlled like horses tamed by the charioteer, a person who is free from pride and flaws.[64] This sort of human being is even better positioned than a deity for enlightenment.

Sakka/Indra

Among the many older gods of Hinduism mentioned in early Buddhist texts, Sakka (Sanskrit Śakra) is perhaps the most important. Sakka is another name for the Hindu deity Indra. In the oldest text of Hinduism, the *Ṛgveda* (ca. 1500–1000 BCE), Indra is a prominent deity associated with thunder and war. Why did the brawny war god of the Hindu Vedas come to play an important part in Buddhism, where he is often referred to as *devānam indo*, "the king of the gods"? The answer to this question is perhaps to be sought in the late Vedic Hindu texts called Upaniṣads, where Indra is reinterpreted as an exemplary wisdom seeker, a student searching for the truth about the nature of the self. The Buddhist Sakka is, like the Upaniṣadic Indra, a seeker after the highest truth. No longer a god of war, he uses his considerable power to protect the *dhamma*, the doctrine of the Buddha.

Although Buddhist texts recognize that Sakka/Indra is a god, several texts mention that he was originally a human being, a notion that is alien to the Hindu tradition. "By vigilance did Indra rise to become lord of the gods. People praise vigilance; thoughtlessness is always deprecated," claims the Buddhist *Dhammapada*.[65] Indra's existence and power is not denied in this text, but his

[64] *Dhammapada* 94, text from Radhakrishnan 1950, 90.
[65] *Dhammapada* 30, text from Radhakrishnan 1950, 68.

position in the Hindu pantheon is explained as the result of his own good character and good *karma* rather than some inherent divine nature. Indra's virtuous nature, which sets a good example for Buddhists to follow, is emphasized in other Buddhist texts as well. The *Saṃyutta Nikāya* of the Pāli canon has several sections devoted to Sakka, who embodies positive qualities such as energy, courage, forbearance, kindness, honesty, and politeness.[66]

The *Dīgha Nikāya* features a long dialogue between Sakka and the Buddha himself.[67] Sakka asks about the causes of desire, malice, happiness and sorrow, equanimity, control over the senses, and good behavior, and comes to understand how good qualities are cultivated and character flaws are overcome. In this dialogue, Sakka is a wisdom seeker who is eager to learn from the Buddha.

Other Hindu gods in Buddhism

Other Hindu deities mentioned in Buddhist texts include the sun god Suriya (Sanskrit Sūrya), the moon god Camdima (Candra), Pajjunna (the Vedic rain god Parjanya), Aggi (Agni, the Vedic god of fire), Varuṇa (the Vedic guardian of cosmic order, later a god of the ocean), the Vedic creator god Prajāpati, the post-Vedic creator god Brahmā (often called Sahampati in Buddhism), Iśāna (Viṣṇu), Viṣṇu's consort Śrī, the goddess of good fortune wand wealth, Yama, the lord of the dead, the ocean god Samudra, and Skanda, the son of the god Śiva. For the most part, these deities function as minor characters in Buddhist texts, extras in the vast cosmic cast that populates the Buddhist universe.

A few deities take on more central roles in Buddhism, however, and in the following, we will take a closer look at some local Buddhist pantheons.

The Buddhist Pantheon of Śrī Laṅkā

The island of Śrī Laṅkā, off India's south-eastern coast, has been an important center of Buddhist culture since the 3rd century BCE. Home to an ancient and still thriving monastic tradition, Śrī Laṅkā offers an interesting example of how local and regional deities are incorporated into Buddhist practice.

According to local beliefs, the island of Śrī Laṅkā itself is protected by four guardian deities ("The Gods of the Four Warrants"). Usually, this group of four includes the gods Viṣṇu, Saman, Vibhīṣaṇa, and Kataragama, although Natha and Pattini are sometimes counted among the four guardians as well. The four deities watch over the Buddhist *dhamma* on the island, although some of them have a non-Buddhist origin.

[66] See for example *Saṃyutta Nikāya* 11: *Sakka-Saṃyuttaṃ*, text in Feer 1884 (1973), 216–240.

[67] *Sakkapañha Sutta, Dīgha Nikāya* 21, text from Rhys Davids and Carpenter 1966, 276–289.

Viṣṇu, as mentioned above, is originally a Hindu deity. Originally a minor sun god in the *Ṛgveda*, Viṣṇu becomes one of the major deities in post-Vedic Hinduism. In the Hindu tradition, Viṣṇu is the benevolent guardian of the universe, who protects the world through his series of incarnations (*avatāras*), which include popular figures such as Kṛṣṇa and Rāma. This guardian function is carried over into Buddhism as well, although Viṣṇu's role is generally less prominent in Buddhism than in Hinduism. Often referred to locally as Upulvan, Viṣṇu is still worshipped in his main shrine in Śrī Laṅkā, the southern port town Devundara (Dondra, "The City of the Gods"), which was once the country's capital. The Viṣṇu temple and its images were unfortunately destroyed by the Portuguese colonial Thome De Sousa D'Arronches and his men in 1587, but many other shrines dedicated to Viṣṇu are still found in temples around the island.

Saman is a deity of more obscure origins. His name is sometimes also rendered as Samanta or Sumana ("the one of good mind"). The 5th-century-CE Buddhist chronicle *Mahāvamsa* mentions a mountain in Śrī Laṅkā called Samantakūta. According to the *Mahāvamsa*, it is the home of a deity called Mahāsumana ("the one of the great good mind").[68] This mountain, which today is also known as Adam's Peak or Śrī Pāda ("The Sacred Footprint"), is an ancient pilgrimage center, well known for a fossilized human footprint embedded in the rock near its peak. Who was the mysterious figure who left a footprint behind in the rock? The *Mahāvamsa* claims that the footprint is that of the Buddha himself, who came to visit Śrī Laṅkā.[69] Christians in the area have long maintained that the footprint is that of Adam (hence the name "Adam's Peak"), while Hindus suggest that it belongs to the god Śiva. Intriguingly, no one claims that Saman, whose ancient dwelling place is supposed to be this very mountain, is responsible for the footprint; rather, he functions merely as a guardian of its location. In later Buddhism, Saman is often identified with the bodhisattva Samantabhadra (see the previous section). Saman's main shrine is at Ratnapura in South-Central Śrī Laṅkā. In art, he is usually depicted accompanied by a white elephant, as is the bodhisattva Samantabhadra. The elephant is often believed to be the same one that appeared to Siddhattha Gotama's mother in her dream in order to announce the birth of the future Buddha.

Vibhīṣaṇa, intriguingly, began as a minor character in the Hindu *Rāmāyaṇa* epic. The *Rāmāyaṇa* tells the dramatic story of the good prince Rāma (a human incarnation of the god Viṣṇu) and his wife Sītā. When Sītā is abducted by Rāvaṇa, the demon king of Śrī Laṅkā, Rāma, goes to Śrī Laṅkā with an army of monkeys, defeats the demon, and rescues Sītā. Vibhīṣaṇa is the brother of the poem's antagonist Rāvaṇa, but while Vibhīṣaṇa is also a demon, he is a righteous demon,

[68] *Mahāvamsa* i.33, text from Geiger 1958. [69] *Mahāvamsa* i.77, text from Geiger 1958.

who opposes his brother's unethical behavior. With Rāma's support, Vibhīṣaṇa is installed as the new king of Śrī Laṅkā at the poem's end. Vibhīṣaṇa is still worshipped today; his main shrine is at Kelaṇiya, a suburb to Śrī Laṅkā's capital Colombo.

Kataragama is both the name of a deity and a town. Identified with Skanda, the son of the Hindu god Śiva, Kataragama is a very popular deity in Śrī Laṅkā. In Hindu mythology, Skanda (also called Kārttikeya) is a young god of war, born of six mothers, who represent the visible stars of the constellation of the Pleiades. He is depicted in art as riding on a peacock. Among the Tamil-speaking Hindus of southern India and Śrī Laṅkā, Kataragama is worshipped under the name Murugan. In North India, Skanda plays a smaller part in Hindu mythology as part of the family that encompasses Śiva, his wife Pārvatī, and their two sons Gaṇeśa and Skanda. In South India, however, Kataragama/Murugan is often worshipped as a powerful deity in his own right, and it is possible that he is originally an ancient South Indian agricultural deity whose worship was later integrated into the cult of Śiva.

Regarded both as a deity and a bodhisattva in Buddhism, Kataragama is associated with emotion and sexuality, and is often worshipped by those who are seeking help in matters of the heart. Kataragama has, according to local mythology, both a wife and a mistress, and messy love affairs is therefore one of his areas of specialization. His wife is the shadowy figure Devasenā ("Divine Army," Tēvānī in Tamil), perhaps a personification of his retinue as a war god. Skanda's mistress in the popular goddess Valli Amma. According to legend, Valli was the young daughter of the chief of the Veddas, the indigenous population of Sri Lanka. When she was twelve, she vowed that she would marry no one but the god Kande Yaka (Kataragama), and the god himself was charmed by her devotion and agreed that it should be so. Often regarded as less scrupulous than deities like Viṣṇu and especially the Buddha himself, Kataragama is approached for help in more worldly matters that would be unsuitable for high moral figures like Viṣṇu. Numerous shrines to Kataragama are found throughout Sri Lanka.

Nātha ("The Lord") is also on occasion included among the four guardian deities of Śrī Laṅkā. His main shrine is at Toṭagamuva in Central Śrī Laṅkā. He is identified with the bodhisattva Avalokiteśvara, although it is possible that he originated as a separate local deity that was later identified with the bodhisattva. The fact that Nātha is also on occasion identified with a different bodhisattva, Maitreya, suggests that this identification is secondary. The worship of Nātha was closely associated with the Sinhala royal family and has been in decline since the end of the Sinhalese monarchy after the signing of the Kandyan Convention in 1815, which accepted British sovereignty over the island.

Last, but certainly not least, among the guardian deities of Śrī Laṅkā is the goddess Pattini. The tragic story of her life is told in the Tamil epic poem *Cilappatikāram* ("The Story of the Anklet," ca. 6th to 9th centuries CE). In this poem, a miraculous baby girl is born from a golden mango, and the king who finds her places her in a golden casket that is floated down the river. She is raised by a couple who find her, and she is named Kannaki (Kannagi). Growing up into a beautiful and virtuous woman, Kannaki marries a man by the name of Kovalan. The two are very happy together until Kovalan leaves Kannaki for a courtesan. Ever devoted, Kannaki forgives him when he finally returns to him, and she gives him her one of her jeweled anklets to sell so he can get started in business. Due to a series of unfortunate misunderstandings, Kovalan is suspected of having stolen the anklet from the queen and is summarily executed by the king. When she learns of her husband's tragic fate, Kannaki shows the king that she has the matching anklet and demonstrates her husband's innocence. In her fury, she curses both the king and the city of Madurai, leaving the king dead and the city in ashes. Afterward, she ascends to heaven with the god Indra. But that is not the end of her story; the royal family of Chera eventually builds a temple to her and call her Pattini ("The Lady") and begin to worship her. And so the virtuous woman who led such a tragic life becomes a goddess. Pattini is regarded as pure, chaste, and virginal, and yet simultaneously as a loving mother.

Pattini is a very popular goddess in Śrī Laṅkā. She is associated with fertility and health and is especially believed to protect against smallpox and other infectious diseases. The anklet of Pattini is believed to protect against disease. Pattini is also associated with rain and agriculture. The most important shrine to the goddess is in Navagamuva in the Sabaragamuva Province in South-Central Śrī Laṅkā. Two of the major rituals for Pattini celebrated in the island are the *gammaḍuva*, a harvest thanksgiving festival, and the *aṅkeḷiya* ("horn game"). Pattini is a goddess and a bodhisattva, but not yet a buddha. Although she is of high moral character, even she will have to be reborn as a male before she can become a fully enlightened buddha. Although Buddhist monks rarely participate in rituals to gods or goddesses in Śrī Laṅkā, they do participate in the *gammaḍuva* festival to Pattini, which is often celebrated in Buddhist temples.[70]

Other popular deities in Śrī Laṅkā include Kālī and Hūniyam. Like Kataragama, these are lower, morally ambiguous deities who can help with worldly problems. Kālī is originally a Hindu goddess, fearsome in appearance and surrounded by images of death and destruction, such as skulls and severed arms. A mother goddess who protects her devotees, Kālī is a fierce slayer of

[70] Obeyesekere 1984, 10.

demons. Hūniyam ("sorcery") was originally regarded as a demon, but through meritorious actions, he gradually became a god. In art, he is surrounded by venomous serpents, and even though he is no longer demonic, he is still associated with more morally ambiguous practices such as magic spells.

Above all the deities in the Sinhalese pantheon, however, is the Buddha. Although he was born a man, he has transcended his humanity and is now regarded as something more than either a man or a god: a buddha. While Sakka is seen as the universal guardian of Buddhism, and Visnu as the guardian of local Buddhism in Śrī Laṅka, the Buddha himself is often regarded as a world ruler (*cakkavattin*) in Śrī Laṅkan Buddhism.[71]

The Buddha is not a god in Śrī Laṅka, but the gods are future buddhas who are not yet fully enlightened but striving to be. Reinterpreting both local deities and Hindu gods originating in India as bodhisattvas, or buddhas-to-be, allows for the integration of popular deities into Theravāda Buddhist practice in Śrī Laṅkā. Hindu gods like Viṣṇu and Skanda are worshipped in Buddhism, but they are not saviors. Rather, they are beings with supernatural powers who can help their worshippers with their little day-to-day problems. By helping people and answering their prayers, the gods themselves accrue good *kamma*, which will help them in their own aspirations toward future buddhahood. The gods themselves are seen as lay followers of the Buddha, and the Buddha is the ultimate source of the power of the gods. All rituals to the gods in Śrī Laṅkā therefore begin with an invocation of the Buddha. In ritual, the Buddha and the higher gods like Viṣṇu and Saman are given "pure" offerings such as flowers, incense, and vegetarian foods, while the lower gods like Kataragama or Kālī are given more impure offerings such as meat.[72] While the Buddha is dead, he is nevertheless venerated with prayers and offerings, and he is believed to be physically present in his relics (*dhātu*). Obeyesekere cites a Sinhalese myth that states that in the "flood that heralds the destruction of this age all the Buddha *dhātu* found in various parts of the world will assemble together through *irdhi* [supernatural ability to float in the air] and the Buddha himself will be refashioned out of these substances. He will then utter a last sermon."[73]

The Tibetan Buddhist Pantheon

A rich Buddhist pantheon is also found in the Tantric forms of Buddhism practiced in Tibet. Tantra (Tibetan *rgyud*) is an esoteric system of meditation and practice whose aim is the transformation of consciousness. Tantra became a public system of thought around 500–600 CE in Northern India, but later became very influential in Tibet as well. Tantric Buddhism is often referred to as

[71] Obeyesekere 1966, 58. [72] Obeyesekere 1966, 10. [73] Obeyesekere 1966, 9.

Vajrayāna (Tibetan *rdo rje'i theg pa*), or the "thunder bolt" path (referring to the thunder bolt as a common symbol of compassion in Tibetan Buddhism).[74] Tantric Buddhism is characterized by an emphasis on esoteric and secret teachings. A person can only learn about Tantra by being initiated by a Tantric teacher. In order to make sure that the teaching does not reach the uninitiated, Tantric texts and artworks use linguistic and visual codes that can only be understood by those who have undergone initiation.

Tantric Buddhism is further characterized by an emphasis on divine revelation. In Mahāyāna Buddhism, there is also a belief in revealed texts, but these texts are located in a heavenly realm somewhere before they are revealed to humans, often through the agency of a bodhisattva. In Tantrism, however, the revelation takes place, not in a heavenly realm, but outside of time and space altogether.

Practitioners of Vajrayāna in Tibet often choose to meditate on deities known as *yidam* ("meditational deity"). A *yidam* is understood to be a manifestation of buddhahood, and meditation on the *yidam* is a way to obtain enlightenment. During meditation, the devotee visualizes the *yidam* in great detail. The purpose of this practice is not to worship a higher being per se, but rather to realize one's own innate buddha nature and purify one's mind.

This "deity yoga" was praised by the 14th-century Tibetan philosopher Tsongkhapa as an essential part of Tantra.[75]

While this deity yoga practice involves an intense focus on the nature and appearance of the deity in question, it is not a form of prayer or a worship of the deity as an entity external to the person. A *yidam* will aid the person in realizing the true nature of the mind, but also serve as a symbol of the enlightened mind itself. The practitioner is therefore not worshipping a being external to themselves, but rather focusing on the *yidam* as symbol of the enlightened state that they hope to achieve. The deity is the focus of meditation and the chanting of mantras, as well as the object of visualization exercises, but ultimately inseparable from the practitioner himself or herself.

In Tantric Buddhism, male buddhas and bodhisattvas are often paired with female partners. Often depicted as *yab-yum* (Tibetan: "father-mother"), or a male and female figure in sexual union, these pairs represent the union of compassion and wisdom. The male figure, usually depicted as more active, represents compassion, while the more passive female figure symbolizes wisdom. Visualizing the *yidam* in union with a partner is regarded as a way to overcome duality.

---

[74] Although it draws extensively on Mahāyāna texts, Vajrayāna is often considered by its adherents to be a separate branch of Buddhism, alongside Theravāda and Mahāyāna.

[75] Powers 2007, 271.

The *yidams* of the Vajrayāna pantheon include buddhas, bodhisattvas, and deities. Some of the buddhas and bodhisattvas are local versions of pan-Mahāyāna figures, while others are unique to Tibet. Tibetan Buddhists revere figures such as the future buddha Maitreya, the bodhisattvas Avalokiteśvara and Mañjuśrī, the goddess Tārā, and the legendary teachers Padmasambhava, Yeshe Tsogyal, and Tsongkhapa. In the meditation on and visualization of these *yidams,* there is often a blurred boundary between buddhas, bodhisattvas, gods, and the practitioner themselves.

Chenrezig (known in Sanskrit as Avalokiteśvara) is one of the most revered and widely worshiped bodhisattvas in the Tibetan Vajrayāna tradition. Chenrezig embodies the compassion of all buddhas and is considered a powerful and compassionate being who actively works to alleviate the suffering of sentient beings. Many Tibetan Buddhist traditions include rituals, prayers, and visualizations focused on invoking Chenrezig's compassion and developing a similar compassion for oneself. The Dalai Lama is considered an incarnation of Chenrezig, but any earnest practitioner can visualize himself or herself as Chenrezig as well.

Jampelyang (Sanskrit Mañjuśrī) is a bodhisattva associated with wisdom. Depicted as wielding a flaming sword that represents the sharpness of wisdom, cutting through delusions and ignorance, as a *yidam* he represents the practitioner's own potential for wisdom.

Jampa (Sanskrit Maitreya) is regarded as the future buddha, the successor to Siddhartha Gautama. Associated with future enlightenment and the eventual arrival of a new buddha to continue his teachings among suffering beings, Jampa embodies the potential for loving kindness.

Tārā (Tibetan: Jetsun Dolma) is a prominent figure in Tibetan Buddhism and is considered variously a bodhisattva, a female buddha, or a goddess. Tārā is not only an important Tantric *yidam;* her cult is widespread among all Tibetans. Functioning as a gentle and benign mother, a protector from harm, and a powerful helper, Tārā is very much a goddess in a theistic sense as well as a *yidam* in Tibet.

Although her worship originated in India, Tārā became more influential in Tibet than anywhere else. According to legend, the 11th-century Indian scholar Atīśa became a Buddhist monk after receiving a vision of Tārā at a young age. After he was invited to come to Tibet to spread the *dharma* there, Atīśa had another vision of Tārā, and she told him that if he did go to Tibet, his own life would be shortened, but he would benefit numerous living beings. Atīśa decided to go, and he brought the worship of the Indian Tantric goddess Tārā with him.[76] Not only did Atīśa's disciples revere Tārā as the highest deity, but so did the

[76] Powers 2007, 157.

14th-century philosopher Tsongkhapa, who became the founder of the Gelug school of Tibetan Buddhism. The worship of Tārā became so popular in Tibet in the centuries that followed that the foreign goddess came to be regarded as the ancestress of the Tibetan people. The 14th-century Tibetan text *The Red Annals* by Tsalpa Kunga Dorjé refers to an old pre-Buddhist Tibetan legend about the Tibetan people being born from a female ogre and a monkey. But in Tsalpa Kunga Dorjé's retelling, the ogress of the legend is identified with Tārā herself, and the monkey with the bodhisattva Chenrezig.[77]

Tārā is often described as the embodiment of compassion and is deeply associated with the compassionate activities of all buddhas. She is known for her swift and compassionate response to the suffering of all sentient beings. Tārā is believed to have various manifestations, each associated with specific qualities and activities. The two main forms of the goddess in Tibet are Green Tārā and White Tārā. Green Tārā is often associated with protection, action, and swift assistance, while White Tārā is associated with longevity, healing, and serenity. Devotion to Tārā is considered a powerful means to cultivate compassion and receive her blessings. Sometimes said to be the consort of the bodhisattva Chenrezig, Tārā is also a powerful independent mother goddess in Tibetan Buddhism.[78]

Padmasambhava, called Guru Rinpoche ("Precious Guru") in Tibetan, is a semi-legendary figure credited with introducing Tantric Buddhism to Tibet in the 8th century CE and establishing the Samye monastery, the first Buddhist monastery in Tibet. Padmasambhava later came to be regarded as a buddha himself, and later hagiographies depict him as born from a lotus flower (his Sanskrit name means "lotus-born") in a lake, a fully formed eight-year-old child. He is said to have conquered local gods and demons in order to establish the Samye monastery and is believed to have buried *termas* (spiritual treasures, which may include texts or images) all over the Tibetan landscape and in the mind of his disciples for later treasure-seekers (*tertöns*) to find. While contemporary scholars of Buddhism are not ruling out that Padmasambahava may have been a historical Indian teacher instrumental in introducing Buddhism into Tibet, the later Tibetan biographies of his life are hagiographies, full of supernatural elements, and over time, he becomes a buddha-figure, ruling over a Pure Land of his own (*zangdok palri*, "The Copper-Colored Mountain").

Yeshe Tsogyal (Ye shes mtsho rgyal; "Queen of the Lake of Knowledge"), Padmasambahava's partner and spiritual consort, is widely revered as a buddha as well. Some Buddhist sources suggest that she was originally one of the queens of the 8th-century king Tri Songdetsen, who invited Padmasambhava

[77] Beyer 1978, 4. [78] See Beyer 1978.

to Tibet, although she is not mentioned in any of the imperial records from the time period and may have been a purely legendary figure. According to her numerous hagiographies, Yeshe Tsogyal became enlightened after studying and practicing for several years with Padmasambhava. Leaving the emperor behind, she traveled around Tibet with Padmasambhava, burying *termas* for future generations to find. In a 17th-century biography by Taksham Nuden Dorje, Yeshe Tsogyal is described as divine from birth. As a young woman, she is pursued by two competing suitors who are prepared to go to war over her, but the emperor Tri Songdetsen intervenes and claims her for himself. As a queen, she meets Padmasambhava and becomes his student and sexual partner, which was seen as scandalous. The king, who was supportive of her relationship with Padmasabhava, pretended to send her into exile, but she traveled and taught with Padmasambhava and eventually acquired both students and new sexual partners of her own.

Another legendary Tibetan teacher revered as something akin to a deity is the 14th-century philosopher Tsongkhapa. Tsongkhapa, also known as Je Tsongkhapa or Lama Tsongkhapa, is the founder of the Gelug school of Tibetan Buddhism. This school emphasizes the study of Buddhist philosophy, particularly the teachings of Indian philosopher Nāgārjuna, and places a strong emphasis on monastic discipline. Tsongkhapa sought to integrate the *sūtrayāna* (teachings based on *sūtras*) and *tantrayāna* (teachings based on tantric practices) aspects of Buddhism. He emphasized the importance of a solid foundation in *sūtra* teachings before engaging in advanced tantric practices. Tsongkhapa was a prolific writer and composed numerous works on various aspects of Buddhist philosophy and practice. His writings cover topics such as Madhyamaka philosophy, ethics, meditation, and the stages of the path to enlightenment. One of Tsongkhapa's most famous works is *The Three Principal Paths*, which outlines the foundational practices of renunciation, *bodhicitta* (the mind of enlightenment), and the correct view of emptiness. This text is widely studied in the Gelug tradition.

Palden Lhamo ("the glorious goddess") is wrathful deity who protects the Buddhist *dharma*. She is regarded as the protector of the Himalayan kingdom of Bhutan but is also widely revered in Tibet and Mongolia. Sometimes associated with the bloodthirsty Hindu goddess Kālī, Palden Lhamo is said to have been married to the evil king of Lanka (Śrī Laṅkā). She made a vow that if she could not convert her husband to Buddhism, she would end his dynastic line. The king not only refused to convert but also raised their son to kill Buddhists. Palden Lhamo therefore killed their son, ate his flesh, and drank his blood before fleeing through Tibet and Mongolia. After death, she was reborn in hell due to the terrible murder of her child, but she eventually managed to flee hell, carrying with her a sword and a bag filled with diseases. After praying to the Buddha, she had a vision of the buddha Vajradhara, who instructed her to change her ways and become the protector of the *dharma*. Palden Lhamo is also the protector of the lineage of the Dalai Lamas. She is at the head of a group of female divinities, the twelve Tenma goddesses, who are said to have been local guardian deities in Tibet before Buddhism, forced by Padmasambhava to promise to protect Buddhism in the country.

Another important female *yidam* in Tibetan Buddhism is Dorje Neljorma (Sanskrit Vajrayoginī). She is considered both a female buddha, as well as a *ḍākinī* (female spirit). Her bright red skin and three eyes represent her blazing spiritual energy and her insight. She is revered in all four schools of Tibetan Buddhism. She is often depicted in sexual union with the wrathful deity Heruka, and their union is said to represent the union of wisdom and skillful means. She is also associated with the Tantric practice of *phowa*, or the transference of consciousness after death. Practitioners visualize the Dorje Neljorma in order for their consciousness to enter a pure land at the moment of death.

But are the Tantric deities really "deities" comparable to, say, the god of monotheistic religions? Not necessarily. As the Tibetan Lama Thubten Yeshe writes:

> Tantric meditational deities should not be confused with what different mythologies and religions might mean when they speak of gods and goddesses. Here, the deity we choose to identify with represents the essential qualities of the fully awakened experience latent within us. To use the language of psychology, such a deity is an archetype of our own deepest nature, our most profound level of consciousness. In tantra we focus our attention on such an archetypal image and identify with it in order to arouse the deepest, most profound aspects of our being and bring them into our present reality.[79]

In other words, the mediational deities of Tantrism, while certainly deities in the sense that they are supernatural beings that are the focus of prayer, ritual, and meditation, *actually represent the potential for awakening within the human worshipper.* A meditational deity such as Nairātymā should not be understood as a divine being external to the worshipper, but rather a symbol of the worshipper's own potential for the realization of non-self.

The Japanese Buddhist Pantheon

The Japanese Buddhist pantheon includes buddhas, bodhisattvas, as well as local deities (*kami*). The *kami* of the indigenous Japanese Shinto religion are spirits that inhabit natural elements, animals, or human beings. Some of the most well-known

[79] Thubten Yeshe 1987, 42.

kami are the sun goddess Amaterasu and the storm god Susanoo. After the introduction of Buddhism to Japan in the 6th century, *kami* also came to play a part in Buddhism. The syncretism between Buddhism and Shinto in Japan from the 8th century onward is referred to as *Shinbutsu-shūgō* ("the blending of *kami* and buddhas"). Many *kami* were identified with Buddhist deities, buddhas, or bodhisattvas.

As in Śrī Laṅkā, buddhas are at the top of the Japanese pantheon, followed by bodhisattvas. The buddhas include the historical Buddha Shakamuni Butsu (Śākyamuni Buddha) and Amida (Amitābha), while popular bodhisattvas include Kannon (Avalokiteśvara, seen as a female figure in Japan), Jizo, and Fugen.

Jizo is particularly associated with compassion, salvation, and the protection of beings, especially those in the afterlife. The name *Jizo* is derived from the Japanese transliteration of the bodhisattva's Sanskrit name, Ksitigarbha, which means "Earth Womb." Jizo is often depicted as a benevolent and compassionate figure who watches over travelers, pilgrims, and, most notably, children. Jizo is often venerated as a protector of children, especially those who have died prematurely or through miscarriage, stillbirth, or abortion. He is believed to guide these souls and ease their suffering.

The bodhisattva Fugen (Samantabhadra in Sanskrit) is widely venerated in Japanese Buddhism. Fugen is revered as the bodhisattva who embodies the practice of meditation and the diligent pursuit of Buddhist virtues. Fugen plays a significant role in the *Avataṃsaka Sūtra* ("Flower Garland *sūtra*"), a central text in Mahāyāna Buddhism. In the *sūtra*, he is often depicted making vows and engaging in practices to benefit sentient beings. Fugen is said to have made ten great vows, expressing his dedication to the welfare of all sentient beings. These vows include the aspiration to honor and serve buddhas, to help beings along the path to enlightenment, and to ensure that all sentient beings attain buddhahood. Fugen is often depicted riding an elephant, emphasizing the stability and tranquility achieved through meditation.

Below the buddhas and bodhisattvas in the Japanese Buddhist pantheon are Wisdom Kings, Heavenly Deities (called *Ten-bu* in Japanese), *Gongen* (incarnations), and monks. The Wisdom Kings (*Vidyārāja* in Sanskrit, *Myōō* in Japanese) are the five guardians of Buddhism: Acala (Japanese: Fudō Myōō), Trailokavijaya (Gōzanze Myōō), Kuṇḍali (Gundari Myōō), Yamāntaka (Daiitoku Myōō), Vajrayakṣa (Kongōyasha Myōō). Acala ("The Immovable One") was originally a minor deity who served the buddha Vairocana, but over time, he came to be seen as a buddha or bodhisattva himself. He is sometimes identified with Vairocana or the buddha Akṣobhya (whose name also means "The Immovable One"). Trailokavijaya ("Victory over the Three Wolds"), is particularly associated with practices related to overcoming obstacles, purifying negativities, and achieving victory over the three realms of existence. The deity is typically depicted with three heads and six arms, holding various implements and weapons symbolizing the power to overcome obstacles and subdue negative forces. Kuṇḍali/Gundari is a wrathful deity that is particularly prominent in the Shingon and Tendai traditions of Japanese Buddhism. He is believed to protect against poison, disease, and disasters. Yamāntaka ("The Conqueror of Death"), also known as Vajrabhairava in Sanskrit, is a wrathful deity considered a fierce manifestation of Mañjuśrī, the bodhisattva of wisdom. Yamāntaka is known for his ability to conquer death and destroy the obstacles on the path to enlightenment. Vajrayakṣa/Kongōyasha is typically depicted holding *vajra* (thunderbolt) weapons, such as a *vajra*-tipped staff (*vajra-daṇḍa*) and a vajra noose (*vajra-pāśa*). The *vajra*, symbolizing indestructible power, is a central attribute in the iconography of Kongōyasha. These wisdom kings are deities who are associated with the four cardinal directions and the center and function as guardians of Buddhism and of the land.

Particularly interesting are the *Gongen*, who are buddhas manifested as *kami,* indigenous deities of Japan. From the 9th century CE onward, *honji suijaku* ("original ground and manifestation") theory of Japanese Buddhism claims that Indian Buddhist deities chose to become incarnated as *kami* in Japan in order to convert the Japanese to Buddhism. According to this theory, *kami* and Buddhist deities and buddhas all share the same fundamental nature (*honji*), while manifesting themselves in different forms (*suijaku*). For this reason, the old Japanese sun goddess Amaterasu was, for example, easily identified with Dainichi Nyorai, which is the Japanese form of the bodhisattva Vairocana.

Other Superhuman Beings in Buddhism

The Eight Legions (Sanskrit *Aṣṭasenā*) are mentioned in Mahāyāna texts as a group of superhuman beings which includes *devas* (gods) and *nāgas* (serpents), *yakṣas* (nature spirits), *gandharvas* (celestial musicians), *asuras* (demigods), *garuḍas* (golden-winged birds), *kiṁnaras* (part-human, part-bird), and *mahoragas* (part-human, part-snakes).

A Yakṣa (Pāli *Yakkha*) is a nature spirit associated with trees, water, vegetation, fertility, and wealth in India. They are featured in Buddhist, Hindu, and Jain mythology. In art, male *yakkhas* are often depicted as short and stout (much like dwarves in European folklore), while the female *yakkhiṇī* (Sanskrit *yakṣiṇī*) is depicted as beautiful, curvy, and seductive. Likely old fertility deities, they are often depicted in Buddhist art.

The serpentine *Nāga* (female Nāginī) is also a benevolent semi-divine creature common to Hinduism and Buddhism. Sometimes they are depicted as completely serpentine, but more often as half-human half-snake. Like Yakkhas, *Nāgas* are frequently depicted in temple architecture, but do not appear to have had an extensive cult.

Collectively, these superhuman beings are, along with the gods, often featured as part of the Buddha's cosmic audience in Mahāyāna texts, listening entranced as he explains the path to enlightenment.

6 The Sacred in Buddhism

While deities are less important in Buddhism than in most other religious traditions, the idea of a higher, numinous reality beyond the realm of human suffering is central to Buddhist doctrine. This section discusses central aspects of Buddhism such as the three jewels (the Buddha, the *dhamma*, and the *sangha),* stūpas, relics, sacred texts, *nibbāna*, and emptiness, and concludes that ideas of the sacred, as a realm set apart from mundane existence, can exist apart from notions of a personal god.

Religion and the Sacred

For several scholars of religion, the concept of the sacred is at the very heart of the definition of religion. The French scholar Émile Durkheim (1858–1917), whose ideas have helped shape the fields of both sociology and religious studies, distinguished between two realms of human experience, the sacred and the profane. For Durkheim, the profane encompasses all the ordinary everyday aspects of life, while the sacred is that which is set apart, revered, and regarded as particularly significant. Durkheim asserted that religion binds individuals together as a social group by collectively affirming and worshipping that which is held to be sacred.[80]

A similar distinction between the sacred and the profane can be found in the works of the Romanian-born scholar of religion Mircea Eliade (1907–1986). For Eliade, as for Durkheim, the sacred is that which is imbued with special significance, as opposed to the everyday world of the profane. While Durkheim sees the sacred as something that is collectively produced by society, Eliade bases his work on the assumption that the sacred is ontologically real, and he refers to the "breaking through" of the sacred into the mundane world as a *hierophany*, a revelation of the sacred.[81] Eliade's concept of hierophany provides a framework for understanding religious experiences and practices as moments of encounter with the sacred. Hierophanies serve to bridge the gap between the human and the divine, offering glimpses of transcendent reality and providing meaning and significance to human existence.

[80] Durkheim 1915 [1912]. [81] See for example Eliade 1959.

Is Buddhism a religion? The answer to that question depends entirely on how one defines "religion." As noted neuroscientist of religion Patrick J. McNamara writes: "Try to define religion and you invite an argument."[82] Although there is no single universally recognized definition of religion, many commonly accepted definitions include a system of beliefs pertaining to higher powers, the sacred, and the meaning of life, a system of rituals and practices that unite people in a community, and a system of guidelines for ethical behavior. Does such a system have to include a belief in a personal god or gods to be defined as a religion? Or can a "higher power" be something less personal and more abstract, like a cosmic order, a life force, or a higher principle?

If religion is defined as a system of beliefs and practices that encompasses the belief in and worship of a personal god, Buddhism may fall outside the scope of the category of religion. But if we draw on Durkheim's and Eliade's view of religion as something closely connected with the notion of the sacred, Buddhism will very much qualify as a religion. In this section, we will focus on some of the most significant expressions of the idea of a sacred reality set apart from our everyday experience in Buddhist traditions.

The Three Jewels

To begin, we will examine three facets of Buddhism that are essential to Buddhist belief and practice: the three jewels (Pāli *ratana-ttaya*, Sanskrit *ratna-traya*). Buddhist devotees declare their commitment to the tradition by declaring that they take refuge in the Buddha, the *dhamma*, and the *sangha.* The Buddha here represents not only the historical founder of the Buddhist tradition, but also the very idea of buddhahood as something the person is aspiring to achieve. The *dhamma* is the teaching of the Buddha, which leads to enlightenment, and the *sangha* is the Buddhist community. What does it mean to "take refuge" in these three things? A refuge (*sarana*) in this case is literally a shelter, something that will protect a person and keep them safe. The three jewels become a refuge for those who are suffering in the world precisely because they provide relief from suffering by facilitating the path to enlightenment: the Buddha by his example, the *dhamma* as an explanation of the path, and the *sangha* as a form of support along the way.

While the Buddha is not regarded as a god, he is nevertheless set apart in Buddhism and regarded as something other than a regular human being. The Buddha represents the potential of any living being to reach enlightenment, and taking refuge in the Buddha therefore means, in one regard, to accept the idea that enlightenment is possible. The teachings of the Buddha point the way to

[82] McNamara 1984, 3.

enlightenment and the liberation from dissatisfaction and suffering, while the community of monks, nuns, and lay practitioners offer support and guidance along the way. The three jewels can therefore be regarded as sacred in Buddhism, not in the sense that they are divine or eternal, but in the sense that they relate to a reality that is free from suffering, apart from the one in which we currently live.

Dhamma or *dharma* is a powerfully loaded term in a South Asian context. The Sanskrit word *dharma* is closely associated with the Brahmanical tradition, where it carries shades of meaning such as "cosmic and moral order," "ritual duty," and "socially sanctioned behavior." In the Brahmanical tradition, a person's *dharma* is determined by caste, gender, and social roles. In Buddhism, the Pāli term *dhamma* and the Sanskrit term *dharma* are used to signify the teachings of the Buddha, as well as morally correct actions or "righteousness." *Dhamma* encompasses such shades of meaning as "truth," "religion," and "Buddhism" itself. But is the *dhamma* itself something eternal? The answer is in one sense no, since there is nothing eternal in Buddhism. And yet, one might argue that the *dhamma* encompasses truthful observations about the suffering of living beings and the path to escaping that suffering. Above all, the *dhamma* provides a framework for understanding the purpose of life and offers guidance on how to live. The Buddha's teachings outline not only the path to end suffering but also guidance for moral conduct for both lay followers and monks and nuns.

The *sangha,* or the Buddhist community itself, is a significant part of the Buddhist society. Durkheim emphasized the presence of a "moral community" in his definition of religion: "A religion is a unified system of beliefs and practices relative to sacred things, that is to say, things set apart and forbidden – beliefs and practices which unite into one single moral community called a Church, all those who adhere to them."[83] While Durkheim's reference to a "Church" is oddly Christian-centered, there can be no doubt that the Buddhist sangha can be defined as a "moral community" that is united by beliefs and practices related to sacred things.

Relics and Stūpas

Both objects and places can be held as sacred in religious traditions, and this is true of Buddhism as well. *Stūpas* are Buddhist shrines or monuments that commemorate the Buddha and his teachings. Some stūpas are constructed at sites that are associated with the Buddha's life, such as the sites of his birth (Lumbini), his enlightenment (Bodh Gaya), his first sermon (Sarnath), or his

[83] Durkheim 1915, 47.

death (Kushinagar). Visiting these shrines serve multiple purposes for devout Buddhists: they inspire deeper thought about the Buddha's path to enlightenment as well as one's own; they foster a sense of community among those gathered at the stūpas, and visits to stūpas for veneration are also believed to generate karmic merit that will positively influence one's future life or lives.

Furthermore, many stūpas are said to contain relics of the Buddha. These relics are physical objects associated with Siddhartha Gautama or other buddhas. Buddhist relics can be divided into three kinds: Bodily relics, *dharma* relics, and mental relics.[84] Bodily relics are physical remains of the Buddha's body, such as bones or teeth, which are believed to have survived cremation. According to Buddhist tradition, after the Buddha's cremation, his remains were divided into eight portions, and relics were enshrined in stūpas across ancient India. These bodily relics are venerated and considered sacred.

Dharma relics are objects associated with the Buddha or other revered figures, such as his alms bowl, robes, or personal possessions. Dharma relics also include objects that are believed to have been touched or used by the Buddha during his lifetime. These relics symbolize the teachings (*dharma*) of Buddhism and serve as reminders of the Buddha's wisdom and compassion.

Mental relics are nonphysical relics that consist of the qualities and virtues cultivated by enlightened beings, such as compassion, wisdom, and equanimity. Practitioners seek to cultivate these mental relics within themselves through meditation, ethical conduct, and spiritual practice.

The veneration of bodily relics and dharma relics at stūpas is a widespread phenomenon in Buddhism. Circumambulating (walking around) the stūpa in a clockwise direction is a common practice during pilgrimage, symbolizing the path toward enlightenment.

The relics are representations of the sacred teachings of the Buddha, and their ultimate power derives from their symbolic significance. Bodily relics, for example, serve as reminders of mortality and of the futility of getting attached to a physical body, while *dharma* relics are reminders of the eightfold path. Nevertheless, there are also popular beliefs in the miraculous power of these relics to heal or bring good fortune or spiritual merit.

But the stūpa is not only a place where relics are stored; they are also themselves symbols of the path to enlightenment. The shape of a stūpa is rich in symbolism; its rounded shape signifies the Buddha's enlightenment, while its spire represents the upward movement from the earthly to the divine. Stūpas can serve as focal points for meditation and contemplation. Practitioners may visualize themselves as the stūpa, embodying its qualities of enlightenment

[84] See Strong 2004.

and wisdom. Meditating near a stūpa is believed to amplify spiritual energy and facilitate insight.

Building stūpas is often a communal endeavor, bringing together Buddhist communities to honor the teachings of the Buddha and commemorate important events or figures in Buddhist history. Stūpas may also be constructed as acts of merit-making, dedicating the positive karma accrued to all sentient beings.

Sacred Texts

As we saw in Section 1, there are several vast Buddhist canons of sacred texts. It is worth noting that Buddhist texts are not only significant because of the ideas they contain; there are also many examples in Buddhist texts themselves of physical copies of texts becoming objects of veneration. Buddhists regard sacred texts not only as repositories of spiritual teachings but also as tangible manifestations of the *dharma* (the Buddha's teachings) and objects worthy of reverence. Buddhists often make offerings to sacred texts as acts of devotion and reverence. Offerings may include flowers, incense, candles, or food placed before the texts as a sign of respect. Devotees may also bow or prostrate before the texts as a gesture of humility and reverence, acknowledging the wisdom contained within them. In some Buddhist traditions, sacred texts are enshrined within special containers or cabinets known as "dhāraṇī pillars" or "scripture halls." These containers are often ornately decorated and may be placed in prominent locations within temples or monasteries. Displaying sacred texts in this manner serves to honor and venerate their importance within the Buddhist tradition. Devotees may travel to monasteries or temples where rare or ancient manuscripts are preserved to pay their respects, make offerings, and seek blessings. Pilgrimage to sacred texts reinforces the connection between believers and the teachings they embody.

Nibbāna

Nibbāna (Sanskrit *nirvāṇa*) is the ultimate "thing set apart" in Buddhism; it represents a reality radically different from all mundane experience. *Nibbāna* is not a "highest principle" like the Hindu *brahman* of the *tao* of Taoism; rather, it is an absence of ill. It is not some sort of divine principle that is the origin of the world, or the substrate of the world (Nyanaponika 1960, vi). The concept of *nibbāna* may not always be interpreted as religious, but it does meet Durkheim's and Eliade's definitions of "the sacred" as something set apart from and transcending mundane existence. It is notable that *nibbāna* is often described in terms that are similar to those that are used to describe divine beings in other religious traditions; *nibbāna* is ineffable and blissful.

Nibbāna is described as an unconditioned reality beyond the realm of conditioned phenomena. It is the ultimate truth or reality that lies beyond the dualities of existence and nonexistence, impermanence and permanence. *Nibbāna* is not subject to arising and passing away like conditioned phenomena but is timeless and deathless.

Emptiness

While the idea of the emptiness of all phenomena is explained in Theravāda Buddhist texts, emptiness (Pāli *suññatā*, Sanskrit *śūnyatā*) itself takes on something of a numinous quality in Mahāyāna Buddhism. In the most fundamental sense, emptiness is a lack of self or essence. In the *Suñña Sutta* (*Samyutta Nikaya* 35), the Buddha explains to his disciple Ānanda what it means that the world is "empty": "It is empty because it is devoid of a self or anything connected to a self."[85] In other words, no things in the empirical world possess any sort of permanent identity; they are fleeting phenomena that come into being due to various causes and conditions, persist for some time, and then cease to exist. There is nothing eternal in the world that we live in.

But emptiness became a significant concept in itself in the *Prajñāpāramitā* (Perfection of Wisdom) *sūtras*, a collection of Mahāyāna Buddhist texts composed between the 1st century BCE and the 1st century CE. All phenomena (*dharmas*) are devoid of self or essence. Emptiness is closely linked to the concept of dependent origination (*pratītyasamutpāda*). According to this teaching, all phenomena arise in dependence on causes and conditions, and they cease when those causes and conditions cease. Emptiness elucidates the interdependent nature of all phenomena, revealing that they lack inherent existence precisely because they arise due to dependent origination.

As we saw in Section 2, *pratītyasamutpāda* (Pāli *paṭiccasamuppāda*) is a fundamental concept in Buddhism. It describes the interconnected nature of all phenomena and explains how the cycle of suffering perpetuates through a chain of causal relations. The causal chain of *pratītyasamutpāda* begins with ignorance, which in turn gives rise to volitional formations (*saṃskāras*), consciousness, name and form, the six sense bases (eye, ear, nose, tongue, body, and mind), contact, desire, grasping, becoming, birth, and aging and death. Human identity is therefore nothing but a snapshot in time of smaller parts of a causal chain that perpetuates suffering in the world. The concept of dependent origination is typically depicted as a twelve-link chain (twelve nidānas) describing the process of birth, aging, death, and rebirth, known as samsara. Each link in the chain arises in dependence on preceding conditions, and the cessation of any

[85] *Suñña Sutta*, *Samyutta Nikaya* 35.85, text from Feer 1894, 54.

link can lead to the cessation of suffering. From this perspective, the boundaries between self and other become blurred, highlighting the illusion of a separate, independent self. Significantly, when ignorance ceases, there will also not be any further birth, death, and rebirth, and no more illusion of a self.

As discussed in Section 2, the Mahāyāna idea of emptiness is further refined in the works of the 2nd-century-CE philosopher Nāgārjuna, the founder of the Madhyamaka school of Buddhist philosophy. Nāgārjuna asserts that all phenomena lack inherent, independent existence or self-nature (*svabhāva*). Nothing exists in and of itself, independent of other causes. Instead, all phenomena are interdependent, arising and ceasing in dependence on other factors, and are thus "empty" of inherent existence. Emptiness is considered the ultimate nature of reality, and understanding it is crucial for attaining liberation (*nirvāṇa*) from suffering.

Following Nāgārjuna, Māhayāna philosophers often discuss emptiness within the framework of the two truths (Sanskrit: *satya*), conventional truth (*samvṛti*), and ultimate truth (*paramārtha*). Conventional truth refers to the relative, everyday understanding of phenomena, while ultimate truth points to their ultimate nature, which is empty of inherent existence. Emptiness is considered the ultimate truth, while conventional reality is seen as interdependent. But is emptiness *something* in itself, or is it merely the fact that all phenomena are empty? While Nāgārjuna does not posit emptiness as something in and of itself (which would imply, perhaps, that emptiness itself possesses a *svabhāva*, which would be inconceivable in his philosophical system), emptiness does over time assume more positive characteristics in Mahāyāna Buddhism.

Wisdom (*prajñā*) in Mahāyāna Buddhism is the direct insight into emptiness, which cuts through the ignorance (*avidyā*) that binds sentient beings to the cycle of death and rebirth. In Mahāyāna Buddhism, emptiness is not a nihilistic concept that negates the conventional world. Rather, it is inseparable from compassion (*karuṇā*) and the bodhisattva path. The realization of emptiness enables bodhisattvas to skillfully engage with the world and alleviate the suffering of sentient beings, understanding the illusory nature of phenomena while compassionately working for their benefit.

Within Tibetan Buddhist Tantra, emptiness is often associated with the idea of the nondual nature of reality. Emptiness and form are seen as two aspects of the same reality, with form arising from and inseparable from emptiness. This view is often encapsulated in the phrase "form is emptiness, emptiness is form." Emptiness in Tantric Buddhism is associated with the transcendental wisdom (*prajñā*) that penetrates the true nature of reality. This wisdom is not merely intellectual understanding but a direct realization of the emptiness of inherent existence. Tantric practices, such as deity visualization, mantra recitation, and ritual, are aimed at cultivating this wisdom and realizing the inseparability of emptiness and form.

Emptiness is, however, reinterpreted in certain forms of Buddhism, such as Tibetan Dzogchen, *shentong*, or the Chinese Chan school, to become a form of primordial awareness. Dzogchen or "Great Perfection" is a tradition within several schools of Tibetan Buddhism that is concerned with the inherent pure, luminous, and pure nature of the primordial mind (*rig pa*). Particularly prominent in the Nyingma school of Tibetan Buddhism as well as in the indigenous Tibetan tradition of Bön, Dzogchen teachings reinterpret emptiness as a primordial awareness present in all living beings that needs to be uncovered. In Dzogchen, emptiness is the ultimate nature of reality. Emptiness is understood as the inherent openness, spaciousness, and nonconceptuality of all phenomena. Emptiness cannot be fully grasped by the conceptual mind but is already present in the pure primordial awareness of *rig pa*. Emptiness is still understood as the interdependence of all things, as in Nāgārjuna's philosophy, but the realization of this cosmic interdependence is itself a form of primordial knowledge common to all living beings.

Shentong is a philosophical approach within Tibetan Buddhism that emphasizes the significance of "other-emptiness" (Tibetan: *gzhan stong*, pronounced *shentong*). This view stands in contrast to the more commonly known *rangtong* view, which emphasizes "self-emptiness" (Tibetan *rang stong*). *Shentong* asserts that while all phenomena are empty of inherent self-nature or essence (*rangtong*), the ultimate reality itself is not empty of its own nature. Thus, the highest reality (Nāgārjuna's paramārtha-satya) while empty of things other than itself, such as phenomenal reality, is ultimately real and possesses an ontological status different from all other things. This other-emptiness is often described as the ultimate nature of reality, which is pure, luminous, and beyond conceptual elaboration. According to *shentong* teachings, the ultimate truth is ineffable and transcends all conceptual constructs. It is not merely an absence of phenomena, but the ground of all being, the ultimate source of wisdom and compassion. *Shentong* emphasizes the primordial purity, luminosity, and innate potential for awakening within all beings.

An influential proponent of *shentong* views was the Tibetan Buddhist monk Dölpopa Sherab Gyaltsen (1292–1361), and these ideas were popular in the Jonang school of Tibetan Buddhism. While the Jonang school was suppressed by the dominant Gelug-pa school under the powerful fifth Dalai Lama, *shentong* ideas are still found in several forms of Tibetan Buddhism, including several lineages of the Kagyu school.

The *rangtong* philosophical view within Tibetan Buddhism, on the other hand, emphasizes the emptiness (*śūnyatā*) of all things, including emptiness itself. Rangtong is often associated with the Madhyamaka tradition of Indian Buddhism, particularly as interpreted by Tibetan scholars like the founder of the Gelug-pa school, Je Tsongkhapa (1357–1419), and has remained the most widely accepted view of emptiness in Tibet.

Emptiness (*kong* or *xukong*) is also a fundamental aspect of Chinese Chan Buddhism. Chan Buddhism emphasizes direct experience over theoretical understanding. Rather than conceptualizing emptiness intellectually, practitioners are encouraged to perceive emptiness directly it through meditation and introspection. This direct experience of emptiness is considered essential for attaining enlightenment. In Chan Buddhism, emptiness is not seen as a separate state to be attained, but rather as the inherent nature of reality that is always present, regardless of whether one is enlightened or not. In this regard, *kong* bears some similarity to the Tibetan concept of *shentong*; there exists a sacred reality that lies outside the boundaries of the phenomenal world.

In Japanese Zen Buddhism, a continuation of the Chinese Chan school, emptiness plays a significant role in understanding the nature of reality, the self, and the path to enlightenment. Zen Buddhism was first introduced to Japan in the 12th century by the Chinese monk Eisai, who founded the Rinzai school of Zen. Another major Zen lineage, Soto Zen, was later established in Japan by the Japanese monk Dogen, who travelled to China to study Zen and brought its teachings back to Japan. Over time, Zen Buddhism became one of the most prominent and influential schools of Buddhism in Japan.

Zen practitioners engage in rigorous meditation practices, such as *zazen* (seated meditation), *koan* study (the study of paradoxical riddles), and mindfulness, to cultivate direct insight into the emptiness of self and phenomena. A central idea in Zen Buddhism is that human beings are trapped in the cycle of death and rebirth not just by their karma, but also by their conventional thinking. The Zen riddles known as *koans* are therefore not questions to be answered in a traditional way, but rather enigmas designed to challenge our conventional ways of thinking. Koans are not meant to be solved through intellectual analysis or logical reasoning. Instead, practitioners are encouraged to engage with the koan on a deeper, intuitive level, allowing the mind to become open and receptive to insight. One of the most well-known *koans* of Japanese Zen Buddhism is simply *mu* (無), which is derived from the Chinese character for emptiness (pronounced *wu* in Chinese). According to one legend, when the Zen master Joshu was asked, "Does a dog have buddha nature?" he simply answered "*Mu.*" By not responding to a yes-or-no question with a yes or a no, the Zen master encouraged his disciples to reject conventional dualistic thinking and gain insight into the boundless, nondual nature of reality. *Mu* is therefore not only a Zen term for emptiness, but itself a gateway to experience that emptiness.

What do these ideas of emptiness mean for the question of whether Buddhism should be classified as a religion or not? When emptiness is understood, as in many forms of Buddhism, not just as an absence of essence, but as a primordial reality that transcends the phenomenal world, accessible to living beings through meditative practices, it is natural to see emptiness as one possible form of the idea of the sacred in Buddhism.

The Sacred without Gods

While we have seen that there are several aspects of Buddhism that can be classified as sacred and set apart from ordinary existence, it is interesting to note that the sacred is not usually associated with deities in Buddhism. Rather, the deities are part of the mundane world and themselves suffering beings in search of the sacred reality that lies beyond the cycle of death and reincarnation. The sacred in Buddhism, then, is not that which relates to gods, but rather that which relates to *nirvāṇa*, or freedom from suffering for all living beings, including the gods.

References

Baggini, Julian. (2003). *Atheism: A Very Short Introduction*. Oxford: Oxford University Press.

Bareau, André. (1969). The Superhuman Personality of Buddha and Its Symbolism in the *Mahāparinirvāṇasūtra* of the Dharmaguptaka. In Joseph Kitagawa and Charles Long, eds., *Myths and Symbols: Studies in Honour of Mircea Eliade*. Chicago: University of Chicago Press, pp. 9–21.

Batchelor, Stephen. (1997). *Buddhism without Beliefs: A Contemporary Guide to Awakening*. New York: Riverhead Books.

Bechert, Heinz. (1966). *Buddhism: A Non-theistic Religion*. New York: George Braziller (repr. 1970).

Bechert, Heinz. (1992). *The Dating of the Historical Buddha: Die Datierung des historischen Buddha*. Göttingen: Vandenhoeck & Ruprecht.

Beyer, Stephan. (1978). *The Cult of Tārā: Magic and Ritual in Tibet*. Berkeley: University of California Press.

Bhattacharya, Vidhushekhara. (1957). *The Yogācārabhūmi of Ācārya Asaṅga: Part 1*. Calcutta: University of Calcutta.

Bullivant, Stephen. (2013). Defining Atheism. In Stephen Bullivant and Michael Ruse, eds., *The Oxford Handbook of Atheism*. Oxford: Oxford University Press, pp. 11–21.

Bullivant, Stephen and Michael Ruse. (2013). Introduction: The Study of Atheism. In Stephen Bullivant and Michael Ruse, eds., *The Oxford Handbook of Atheism*. Oxford: Oxford University Press, pp. 1–7.

Cabezón, José. (2006). Three Buddhist Views of the Doctrine of Creation and Creator. In Perry Schmidt-Leukel, ed., *Buddhism, Christianity, and the Question of Creation: Karmic or Divine?* Aldershot: Ashgate, pp. 33–46.

Carpenter, Joseph Estlin. (1911). *The Dīgha Nikāya: Vol. II*. London: Luzac (repr. 1960).

Chalmers, Robert. (1896). *The Majjhima Nikāya: Vol. II (Pali Text Society 61)*. London: Routledge & Kegan Paul (repr. 1977).

Chalmers, Robert. (1932). *Buddha's Teachings: Being the Sutta-nipāta or Discourse-Collection*. Oxford: Oxford University Press (repr. Cambridge, Mass.: Harvard University Press, 1978).

Chemparathy, George. (1968–69). Two Early Buddhist Refutations of the Existence of Īśvara as the Creator of the Universe. *Wiener Zeitschrift für die Kunde Süd- und Ostasiens* 12–13: 85–100.

Cheng, Hsueh-Li. (1976). Nagārjuna's Approach to the Problem of the Existence of God. *Religious Studies* 12.2: 207–216.

Cliteur, Paul. (2009). The Definition of Atheism. *Journal of Religion & Society* 11: 1–23.

Collins, Steven. (1998). *Nirvana and Other Buddhist Felicities: Utopias of the Pali Imaginaire*. Cambridge: Cambridge University Press.

Collins, Steven. (2010). *Nirvana: Concept, Imagery, Narrative*. Cambridge: Cambridge University Press.

Dharmapala, Thera K. (1958). *Universal Religion or Religion without God*. Colombo: Maha Bodhi Press.

Dharmasiri, Gunapala. (1974). *A Buddhist Critique of the Christian Concept of God*. Colombo: Lake House.

Durkheim, Émile. (1915). *The Elementary Forms of the Religious Life* (Joseph Ward Swain, Trans.). New York: Macmillan (Original work published 1912).

Dutt, Nalinaksha. (1934). *The Pañcaviṁśatisāhasrikā Prajñāpāramitā, in Sanskrit and English*. London: Luzac.

Dworkin, Ronald. (2013). *Religion without God*. Cambridge, MA: Harvard University Press.

Eliade, Mircea. (1959). *The Sacred and the Profane*. New York: Harcourt.

Fausbøll, Viggo. (1877). *The Jātaka Together with Its Commentary: Vol. I*. London: Trübner.

Fausbøll, Viggo. (1891). *The Jātaka Together with Its Commentary: Vol. V.* London: Kegan Paul Trench Trübner.

Fausbøll, Viggo. (1896). *The Jātaka Together with Its Commentary: Vol. VI*. London: Kegan Paul Trench Trübner.

Feer, Léon. (1888). *The Saṃyutta-Nikāya: Part II: Nidāna-vagga* (repr. London: Luzac, 1970).

Feer, Léon. (1890). *The Saṃyutta-Nikāya: Part III: Khandha-vagga* (repr. London: Routledge & Kegan Paul, 1975).

Feer, Léon. (1894). *The Saṃyutta-Nikāya: Part IV: Salāyatana-vagga*. London: Henry Frowde.

Fozdar, Jamshed. (1973). *The God of Buddha*. New York: Asia Publishing House.

Frauwallner, Erich. (1951). *On the Date of the Buddhist Master of the Law Vasubandhu*. Rome: IsMeo.

Frauwallner, Erich. (1958). *Die Philosophie des Buddhismus*. Berlin: Akademie-Verlag.

Geiger, Wilhelm. (1958). *The Mahāvaṃsa*. London: Luzac.

Glasenapp, Helmuth von. (1966). *Buddhism: A Non-theistic Religion* (Irmgard Schloegl, Trans.). New York: George Braziller.

Gokhale, Vasudeva V. (1946). The Text of the *Abhidharmakośakārikā* of Vasubandhu. *Journal of the Bombay Branch of the Royal Asiatic Society, New Series* 22: 73–102.

Gombrich, Richard and Gananath Obeyesekere. (1988). *Buddhism Transformed: Religious Change in Sri Lanka*. Princeton: Princeton University Press.

Griffiths, Paul J. (1994). *On Being Buddha: The Classical Doctrine of Buddhahood*. Albany: State University of New York Press.

Hardy, Edmund. (1900). *The Aṅguttara-Nikāya* (repr. London: Luzac for the Pali Text Society, 1958).

Harrison, Paul and John McRae. (1998). *The Pratyutpanna Samādhi Sūtra and the Śūraṅgama Samādhi Sūtra*. Berkeley: Numata Center.

Harvey, Peter. (2019). *Buddhism and Monotheism*. Cambridge: Cambridge University Press.

Hayes, Richard. (1988). Principled Atheism in the Buddhist Scholastic Tradition. *Journal of Indian Philosophy* 16.1: 5–28.

Jaini, Padmanabh S. (1974). On the *sarvajñatva* (omniscience) of Mahavira and the Buddha. In Lance Cousins, Arnold Kunst, and Kenneth Roy Norman, eds., *Buddhist Studies in Honour of I. B. Horner*. Dordrecht: D. Reidel, pp. 71–79.

Jootla, Susan Elbaum. (1997). *Teacher of the Devas: The Buddha's Relationship with the Gods*. Kandy: Buddhist Publication Society.

Joshi, L. R. (1966). A New Interpretation of Indian Atheism. *Philosophy East and West* 16: 189–206.

Kimura, Takayasu. (1929). The Date of Vasubandhu Seen from the Abhidharmakośa. In Charles Rockwell Lanman, ed., *Indian Studies in Honor of Charles Rockwell Lanman*. Cambridge, MA: Harvard University Press, pp. 89–92.

Lamotte, Étienne. (1944). *Le traité de la grande vertu de sagesse, Vol. 1*. Louvain: Bureaux du Muséon.

Lancaster, Lewis. (1979). Buddhist Literature: Its Canons, Scribes, and Editors. In Wendy Doniger, ed., *The Critical Study of Sacred Texts*. Berkeley: University of California Press, pp. 215–229.

La Vallée Poussin, Louis de. (1913). *Mūlamadhyamakakārikās (Mādhyamikasūtras) de Nāgārjuna avec la Prasannapadā Commentaire de Candrakīrti*. St.-Pétersbourg: Académie imperiale des sciences (repr. Osnabruck: Biblio Verlag, 1970).

Malalasekara, Gunapala Piyasena. (1937). *Dictionary of Pāli Proper Names*. London: John Murray.

Martin, Michael. (2007). General Introduction. In Michael Martin, ed., *The Cambridge Companion to Atheism*. Cambridge: Cambridge University Press, pp. 1–7.

McNamara, Patrick. (1984). *Religion, North American Style*. Belmont: Wadsworth.

Morris, Richard. (1885). *The Anguttara-nikāya: Part I* (repr. London: Luzac, 1961).

Morris, Richard. (1888). *The Anguttara-nikāya: Part II* (repr. London: Luzac, 1955).

Nyanaponika, Thera. (1960). *Buddhism and the God-Idea: Selected Texts*. Kandy: Buddhist Publication Society.

Obeyesekere, Gananath. (1966). The Buddhist Pantheon in Ceylon and Its Extensions. In Manning Nash, ed., *Anthropological Studies in Theravada Buddhism*. New Haven: Yale University Press, pp. 1–26.

Obeyesekere, Gananath. (1984). *The Cult of the Goddess Pattini*. Chicago: University of Chicago Press.

Powers, John. (2007). *Introduction to Tibetan Buddhism*. Ithaca: Snow Lion.

Pyysiäinen, Ilkka. (2003). Buddhism, Religion, and the Concept of God. *Numen* 50.2: 147–171.

Quack, Johannes. (2016). India. In Stephen Bullivant and Michael Ruse, eds., *The Oxford Handbook of Atheism*. Oxford: Oxford University Press, pp. 651–664.

Radhakrishnan, Sarvepalli. (1950). *The Dhammapada* (repr. Delhi: Oxford University Press, 1996).

Radner, Rebecca. (1993). The Lotus-Born: The Life Story of Padmasambhava. *Tricycle*. Online at https://tricycle.org/magazine/the-lotus-born-the-life-story-padmasambhava/.

Rewatadhamma, Ashin. (1969). *Buddhaghosācariya's Visuddhimaggo, with Paramatthamañjūsāṭīkā of Bhadantācariya Dhammapāla: Vol. 1*. Vārāṇasī: Vārāṇaseya saṁskṛtaviśvavidyālaya.

Rhys Davids, Thomas William. (1963). *Tevijja Sutta: A Discourse of the Buddha on the Path to God*. Kandy: Buddhist Publication Society.

Rhys Davids, Thomas William, and Joseph Estlin Carpenter. (1890). *The Dīgha Nikāya: Vol. I*. London and Boston: The Pali Text Society (repr. Routledge & Kegan Paul, 1975).

Rhys Davids, Thomas William, and Joseph Estlin Carpenter. (1903). *The Dīgha Nikāya: Vol. II*. London: Luzac (repr. 1966).

Skilton, Andrew. (2013). Buddhism. In Stephen Bullivant and Michael Ruse, eds., *The Oxford Handbook of Atheism*. Oxford: Oxford University Press, pp. 337–350.

Spivak, Gayatri C. (1999). *A Critique of Postcolonial Reason: Toward a History of the Vanishing Present*. Cambridge, MA: Harvard University Press.

Stcherbatsky, Theodore. (1923). *The Central Conception of Buddhism and the Meaning of the Word "Dharma."* London: Royal Asiatic Society (repr. Delhi: Motilal Banarsidass, 1974).

Strong, John S. (2004). *Relics of the Buddha*. Princeton: Princeton University Press.

Thomas, Frederick William. (1903). Notes from the Tanjur. *The Journal of the Royal Asiatic Society of Great Britain and Ireland* 35: 345–354.

Trenckner, Vilhelm. (1880). *Milindapañho*. London: Williams and Norgate.

Trenckner, Vilhelm. (1888). *The Majjhima Nikāya: Vol. I*. London: Routledge & Kegan Paul (repr. 1979).

Wallace, Vesna. (2001). *The Inner Kalacakratantra: A Buddhist View of the Individual*. Oxford: Oxford University Press.

Williams, Paul. (2008). *Mahāyāna Buddhism: The Doctrinal Foundations*. 2nd ed. London: Routledge.

Wright, Dale Stuart. (2009). *The Six Perfections: Buddhism and the Cultivation of Character*. Oxford: Oxford University Press.

Yeshe, Thubten. (1987). *Introduction to Tantra: A Vision of Totality*. London: Wisdom.

Cambridge Elements

The Problems of God

Series Editor

Michael L. Peterson

Asbury Theological Seminary

Michael L. Peterson is Professor of Philosophy at Asbury Theological Seminary. He is the author of *God and Evil* (Routledge); *Monotheism, Suffering, and Evil* (Cambridge University Press); *With All Your Mind* (University of Notre Dame Press); *C. S. Lewis and the Christian Worldview* (Oxford University Press); *Evil and the Christian God* (Baker Book House); and *Philosophy of Education: Issues and Options* (Intervarsity Press). He is co-author of *Reason and Religious Belief* (Oxford University Press); *Science, Evolution, and Religion: A Debate about Atheism and Theism* (Oxford University Press); and *Biology, Religion, and Philosophy* (Cambridge University Press). He is editor of *The Problem of Evil: Selected Readings* (University of Notre Dame Press). He is co-editor of *Philosophy of Religion: Selected Readings* (Oxford University Press) and *Contemporary Debates in Philosophy of Religion* (Wiley-Blackwell). He served as General Editor of the Blackwell monograph series Exploring Philosophy of Religion and is founding Managing Editor of the journal *Faith and Philosophy*.

About the Series

This series explores problems related to God, such as the human quest for God or gods, contemplation of God, and critique and rejection of God. Concise, authoritative volumes in this series will reflect the methods of a variety of disciplines, including philosophy of religion, theology, religious studies, and sociology.

Cambridge Elements

The Problems of God

Elements in the Series

God, Religious Extremism and Violence
Matthew Rowley

C.S. Lewis and the Problem of God
David Werther

God and Happiness
Matthew Shea

God and the Problem of Epistemic Defeaters
Joshua Thurow

The Problem of God in Jewish Thought
Jerome Gellman With Joseph (Yossi) Turner

The Trinity
Scott M. Williams

The Problem of Divine Personality
Andrew M. Bailey and Bradley Rettler

Religious Trauma
Michelle Panchuk

Embodiment, Dependence, and God
Kevin Timpe

The Problem of God in Thomas Reid
James Foster

God and Non-Human Animals
Simon Kittle

The Problem of God in Buddhism
Signe Cohen

A full series listing is available at: www.cambridge.org/EPOG

www.ingramcontent.com/pod-product-compliance
Ingram Content Group UK Ltd.
Pitfield, Milton Keynes, MK11 3LW, UK
UKHW021842030325
455810UK00016B/772

9 781009 269186